PERCUSSION REPAIR AND MAINTENANCE

A PERFORMER'S TECHNICAL MANUAL

by **MARK P. BONFOEY**

Edited by **ANTHONY J. CIRONE**

EL 03285

DEDICATION

This book is dedicated to my parents; for their direction and guidance.

Mark Bonfoey is a free-lance percussionist in the San Francisco Bay Area, performing with the symphonies of Monterey, San Jose, and Oakland. He holds Performance Degrees from the University of South Dakota, and San Jose State University, with additional studies in Gamelan and Composition with Lou Harrison. As the founder and owner of MAR-BON PERCUSSION, he is responsible for repair and fabrication of custom percussion equipment and accessories for professionals across the country. He is also Percussion Instructor at Santa Clara University, Santa Clara, California.

*** INTRODUCTION ***

As musicians, we express our art-form through a variety of mediums. Whatever path a performer chooses, certain tools or instruments need to be implemented in order to create a musical setting.

As percussionists, these tools come in many varieties and sizes. No longer can we specialize on one instrument; to be a total performer, a high level of proficiency must be attained on all the percussion instruments. An on-going obsession for the percussionist is the collection of instruments and in order to sound our best, the equipment must be maintained in good working condition.

It is with a feeling of gratitude towards my colleagues that I am able to share solutions to equipment maintenance, and to learn from their experiences. This book was inspired because of their sharing.

M.P.B.

Illustrations by Mark P. Bonfoey

TABLE OF CONTENTS

*** TIMPANI ***

Timpani are mechanically refined, tunable instruments, requiring a certain amount of structural knowledge for proper performance. The main sections of each timpani include:

1. Head
2. Bowl
3. Carriage
4. Pedal

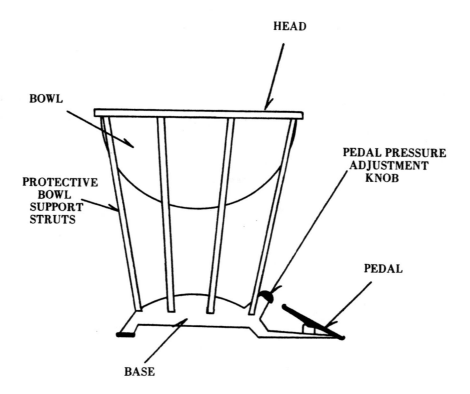

Most of the maintenance involved on timpani will encompass these four main areas.

*** RECONDITIONING THE OLD HEAD ***

Correct care and maintenance of timpani heads are most important for proper pitch and tone. A worn head or one that is not in balance will distort the tone. Because timpani are the primary tunable membrane instruments, nothing is more detrimental to their sound than a problem with the head.

As with other drum heads, dents will start to surface after use. Proper use of felt timpani mallets will not cause any damage. However, with the common use of wooden beaters, the life of the timpani head is dramatically reduced.

Under normal playing conditions, heads should be changed every six months to one year.
In certain situations where the head is not too badly damaged, the dents in the head may be ironed out.
To remove the dents from the head, simply use a standard iron in the manner described below.

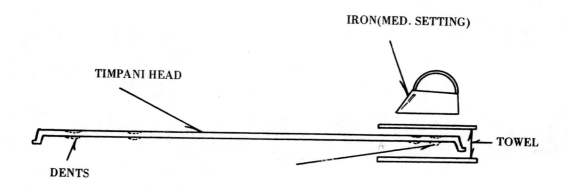

It is also possible to refit a used timpani head on another drum by ironing the collar made by the previous drum. This is illustrated below:

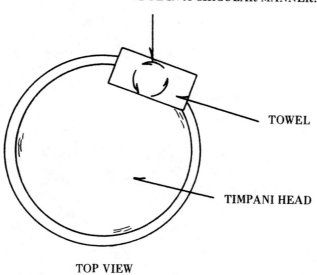

TOP VIEW

*** REMOVING A TIMPANI HEAD ***

Head replacement is a bit more difficult on timpani than on a snare or bass drum. The following steps are recommended for removal of the old head:

1.   Face the drum in playing position and push the heel of the pedal completely to the floor.

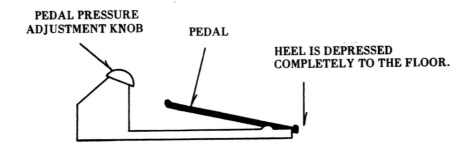

PEDAL PRESSURE ADJUSTMENT

MANY TIMPANI COME EQUIPPED WITH THIS PEDAL PRESSURE ADJUSTMENT. A COMMON DRUM KEY IS INSERTED INTO THE HOLE PROVIDED, TURNED CLOCKWISE TO INCREASE THE PEDAL PRESSURE, AND THEN COUNTER-CLOCKWISE TO DECREASE THE PRESSURE.

2.   Hold the pedal down (as illustrated above,) and begin to remove the head in a symmetrical pattern by loosening the T-knobs or by using a timpani key.

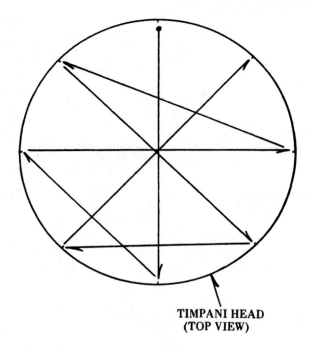

TIMPANI HEAD
(TOP VIEW)

3.   As the lugs are being loosened, the toe of the pedal can gradually be released. If the foot is removed all at once from the pedal, the pedal will slam forward, damaging it or even completely snapping it in two.

4.   Once the pressure has been released, the foot may be removed from the pedal.

5.   The counterhoop and head may now be removed.

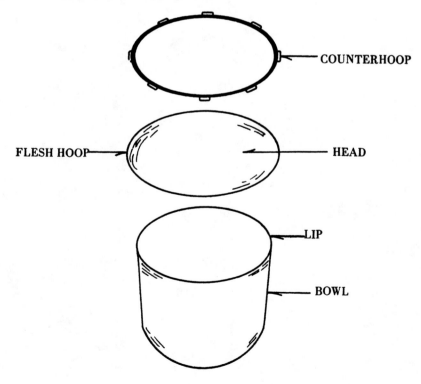

Inspect the lip of the bowl to see if any irregularities are obvious. Any imperfections in the lip should be removed by a competent machinist. A perfect surface on the lip is crucial for perfect intonation.

Figure A indicates how the lip of the bowl would appear if an imperfection were evident. Figure B shows how the lip should appear when it has a perfect angle. In order for the head to ring a true tone, it must rest evenly around the perimeter of the bowl. If the head does not seat properly, it will pull unevenly and cause some distortion with intonation.

A small wedge may be used on the inside of the lip (figure B). The wedge must have the identical angle as the inside angle of the lip. A machine shop will be able to supply or make such a wedge.

Tap the wedge slowly from the inside of the bowl until the original shape of the lip is attained. This process is difficult and should be used only for minor repairs. During this process, turn the bowl upside down so the wedge can be hammered in a downward fashion. It is much easier if there are two people available for this job.

FIGURE A

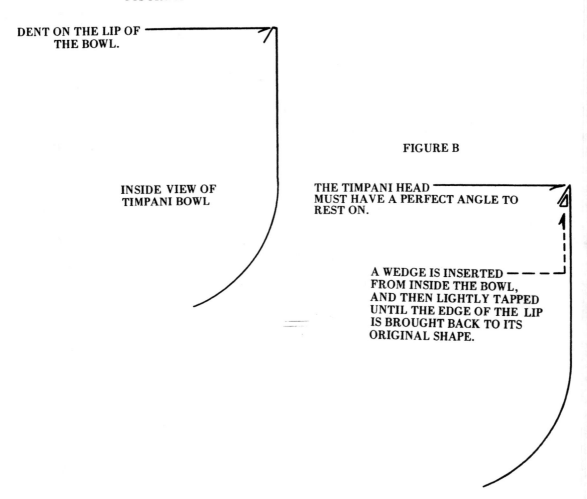

DENT ON THE LIP OF
THE BOWL.

INSIDE VIEW OF
TIMPANI BOWL

FIGURE B

THE TIMPANI HEAD
MUST HAVE A PERFECT ANGLE TO
REST ON.

A WEDGE IS INSERTED
FROM INSIDE THE BOWL,
AND THEN LIGHTLY TAPPED
UNTIL THE EDGE OF THE LIP
IS BROUGHT BACK TO ITS
ORIGINAL SHAPE.

If the lip is in bad shape, it is recommended that the bowl be sent to a competent machinist or returned to the original factory where the proper equipment is available.

*** REMOVING DENTS IN THE BOWL ***

Dents in the timpani bowl are very common. Because timpani are continually being moved from one rehearsal to another, the bowls are susceptible to damage. These dents can be removed from the inside by tapping the dent with a small, rubber hammer. Hold a block of wood against the outside of the shell (over the dent) to prevent over-pounding the dented area. This also helps maintain the metal in its original shape.

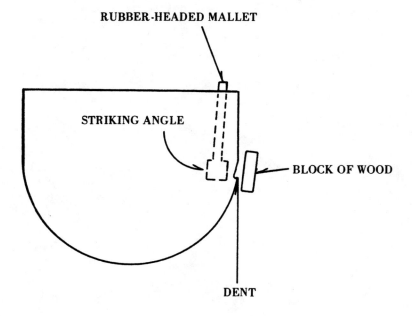

REMOVING DENTS FROM THE
TIMPANI BOWL

RUBBER-HEADED MALLET

STRIKING ANGLE

BLOCK OF WOOD

DENT

Pounding out dents is a slow process. It must be done with small, even strokes. The bowl is important for tone production, so it must be kept in good shape.

*** CLEANING AND CHECKING FOR RATTLES ***

Clean any dirt or dust from the inside of the bowl. The apparatus joining the pedal to the lugs is called the "spider." The spider is located on the inside of the bowl or immediately below. If rattling occurs where the arms meet the center hub, then isolate these two sections from each other.

" SPIDER"

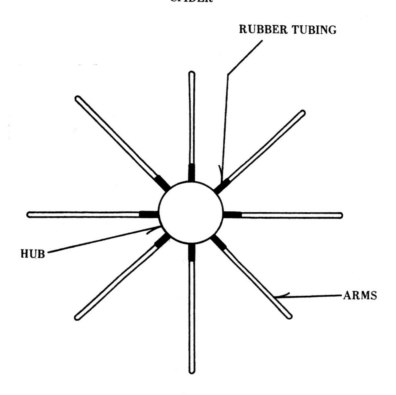

TOP VIEW

Attach a piece of rubber tubing where the two sections are joined. Split the tubing with a razor or knife, slip it around the rod, and slide it up against the center hub. Several layers of electrician's tape will also suffice.

Clean around the lip of the bowl several times with a small piece of steel wool. This will remove any deposits that might have accumulated. Following this, wipe the lip clean with a piece of cloth. Repeat this process on the metal counterhoop.

*** MOUNTING THE HEAD ***

The head is now ready to be put on. Center it so the backbone is at an angle to the beating spot as pictured. A light layer of paraffin wax on the lip of the bowl will help seat the head. (The use of a wax is not necessary and may be more trouble than a benefit. Wax attracts dirt and dust and may cause squeaking noise as it dries.) An alternative to paraffin wax is teflon tape (available at hardware stores).

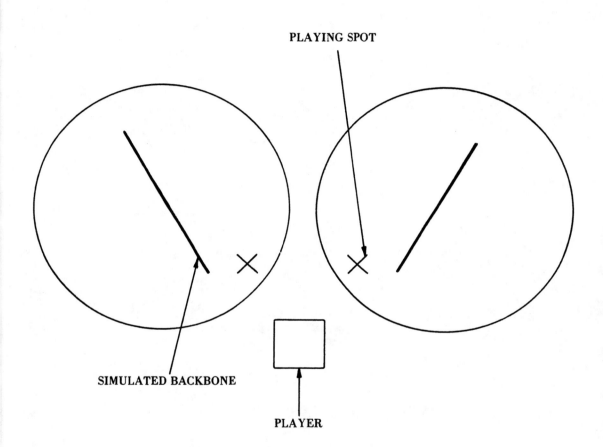

Place the counterhoop over the head and rethread each lug by hand until all are at a uniform tightness. If the lug seems stiff as it is being tightened, remove it from the drum and apply a small amount of petroleum jelly to the threads.

Depress the heel of the pedal completely to the floor and tighten each lug two or three half turns with the key. The pedal will gradually return to its normal tension. At this point, the foot can be removed. The head is now ready to be tuned.

13

*** TUNING THE TIMPANI HEAD ***

The following procedures are recommended for tuning the timpani head:

1. The heel of the pedal must be depressed during this process to remove tension from the head.
2. After each lug has been hand-tightened, make whatever adjustments are necessary to eliminate any wrinkles which may appear on the head.
3. At this point, the head should have a very low but good tone. Turn each rod with the tuning key, rotating opposite points in the same manner as they were removed.

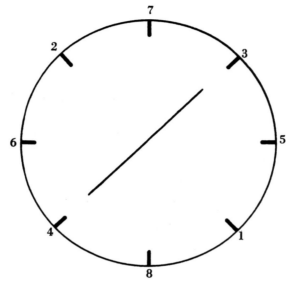

4. Strike the head at the normal beating spot and listen to the pitch. Then strike the drum at each tuning rod and match the pitch of the original spot by tightening or loosening the rod.
5. Press the pedal to a higher pitch and repeat the process.
6. Allow the drum to set in a warm room for a few hours before continuing to fine-tune the head. It is easier to fine tune a drum with the timpani tuned to a high pitch, simply because the higher pitches are easier to hear.
7. If an extended range is needed on the drum, tighten or loosen the entire head. Do not make large adjustments with the fine-tuning key.

Listed below are the normal ranges for the standard set of four timpani. It is possible to tune each drum higher or lower by approximately 1/2 step.

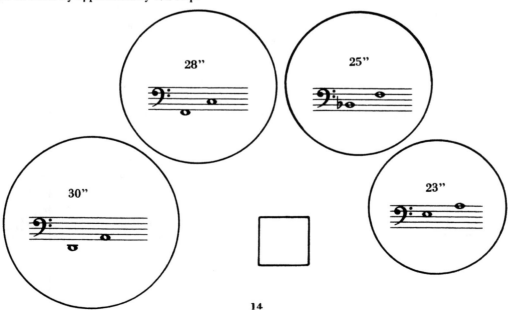

Changing the heads on a Dresden timpani requires a slightly different approach. The most common of the Dresden model timpani are: Goodman, Hinger, Walter Light and Ringer.

Before removing the old head, a brace must be wedged between the spider and base of the drum. A stage weight or 4"x4" block of wood works fine. This brace is used to prevent the spider from completely separating from the drum. Continue the replacement of the head as described on the previous pages. After tightening the new head, the brace may be removed.

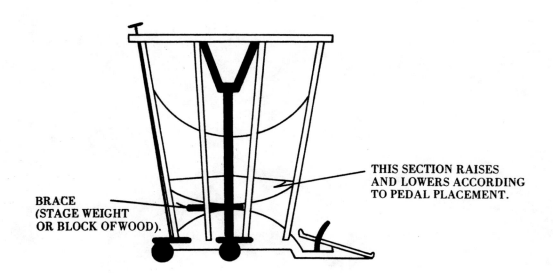

BRACE
(STAGE WEIGHT
OR BLOCK OF WOOD).

THIS SECTION RAISES
AND LOWERS ACCORDING
TO PEDAL PLACEMENT.

FINE-TUNING KEY

...e-tuning key is extremely helpful in attaining a pure and accurate tone. However, they do present problem at times because they tend to rattle. Even though many have a 'wing nut' which tightens them to the shaft, they still have a tendency to vibrate loose while performing.

A good solution is to put a thin layer of duct tape or moleskin on the inside of the key head to isolate the metal key from the shaft. Another solution is to remove the key during performance. Have it nearby, however, to make adjustments as necessary.

TIMPANI FINE-TUNING KEY

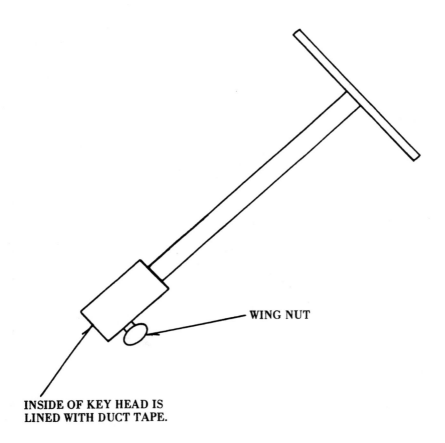

WING NUT

INSIDE OF KEY HEAD IS
LINED WITH DUCT TAPE.

Another suggestion for keeping the heads in perfect tune is to replace all T-knobs with regular lugs which can be tightened by a key. Although the head can be adjusted faster with the T-knobs they are also more likely to be accidentally turned by bumping and moving. This will create havoc with intonation.

It is also easier to perform with T-knobs out of the way; particularly with fast crossing passages.

*** ADJUSTING THE PEDAL TENSION ***

The tension-adjusting knob, found on the base of the timpani, will not always be adjusted for the proper range. If the heel of the pedal will not stay down for low notes, or the toe position will not hold high notes, then adjustment of the knob is needed.

Turning the knob counter-clockwise will lower the heel adjustment and produce notes in the lower range. Turning the knob clockwise will raise the toe position and produce notes in the higher range.

PEDAL PRESSURE ADJUSTMENT
KNOB

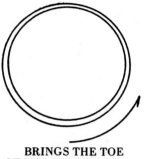

BRINGS THE TOE
OF THE PEDAL BACK

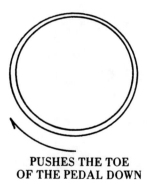

PUSHES THE TOE
OF THE PEDAL DOWN

If this has been attempted and the pedal is still out of adjustment, check the following:

    1.   The timpani may be out of its normal playing range. Refer to the chart on page 13 for the proper range.

    2.   The timpani head may be too old and stretched beyond its ability to hold the normal range. If this is the case, replace the head.

*** A SQUEAKY PEDAL ***

Occasionally a squeak in the pedal occurs. When this happens, apply a small amount of powdered graphite at the point of the noise. Since the pedal is usually grease packed, do not use oil. It will tend to break down the grease, thus compounding the problem. Sparingly apply the powdered graphite. Avoid spilling this messy substance over other areas of the drum or floor.

If the drum rims touch each other while performing, buzzing will result. Move them apart, securing the position by braking the wheels.

*** TIMPANI MUTES ***

Timpani mutes are a necessary part of the timpanist's equipment. Besides being called for in music literature, conductors occasionally ask for a mute to be used for special situations (Ex. to cut down on resonance).

Timpani mutes are easy to construct, and one should be made for each drum. Two pieces of soft felt cut in a three or four-inch circle will be needed for each mute. Fill each of the two pieces of felt with a small amount of fine "buck-shot" and sew the edges together. Lightly stitch across the middle of the mute to keep the pellets from gathering to one side. Then sew an eight-inch loop of heavy string to one side of the mute. This will be used to attach it to the timpani.

TIMPANI MUTE

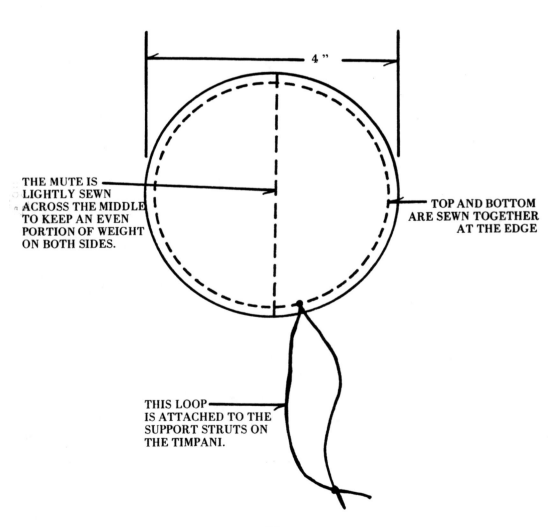

4 "

THE MUTE IS LIGHTLY SEWN ACROSS THE MIDDLE TO KEEP AN EVEN PORTION OF WEIGHT ON BOTH SIDES.

TOP AND BOTTOM ARE SEWN TOGETHER AT THE EDGE

THIS LOOP IS ATTACHED TO THE SUPPORT STRUTS ON THE TIMPANI.

*** MOVING THE TIMPANI ***

Now that the timpani have been finely adjusted and are ready for performing, what happens if they need to be moved? If the drum is moved improperly, all previous efforts will have been in vain. The following diagram shows where to correctly grip the drum while moving. This insures the head will not be pulled to one side. Do not allow the pedal to touch the ground as the drum is being moved.

MOVING TIMPANI

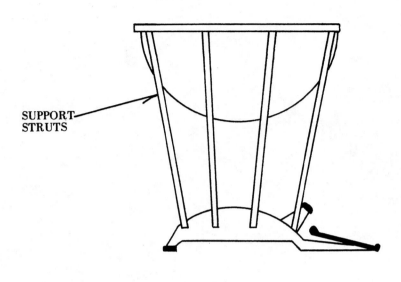

SUPPORT
STRUTS

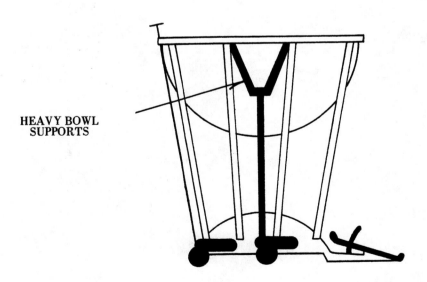

HEAVY BOWL
SUPPORTS

TO INSURE THAT THE HEAD STAYS IN FINE ADJUSTMENT, THE TIMPANI
MUST BE PULLED WHERE INDICATED ABOVE.

*** COVERING THE TIMPANI ***

Timpani should be covered with a large plywood circle or drop cloth when not in use. Cut the plywood circle slightly smaller than the rim of the drum. Attach two ties at opposite edges which will secure the cover to the timpani. Glue a layer of felt to the bottom side of the cover to prevent the wood from touching the head.

TIMPANI COVER
(BOTTOM VIEW)

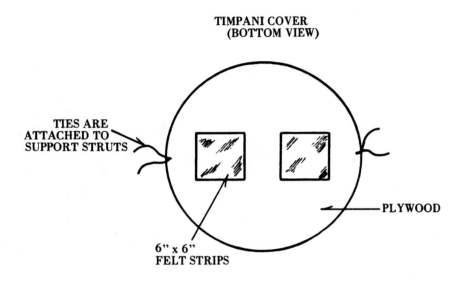

TIES ARE
ATTACHED TO
SUPPORT STRUTS

PLYWOOD

6" x 6"
FELT STRIPS

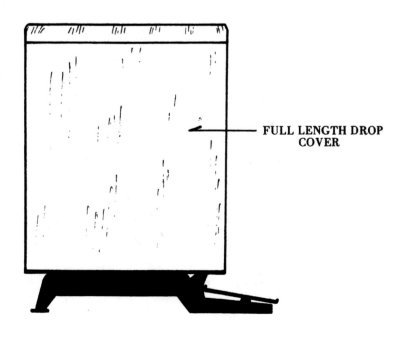

FULL LENGTH DROP
COVER

EXTENDED TIMPANI SET-UPS
FIVE DRUMS

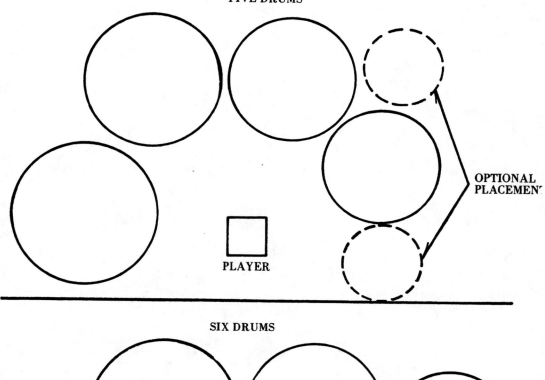

OPTIONAL
PLACEMENT

PLAYER

SIX DRUMS

PLAYER

*** BASS DRUM ***

The following chapter discusses ideas for playing and maintaining the bass drum. The large amount of sound produced by the bass drum accounts for many of the problems in caring for it.

*** BASS DRUM HEADS ***

Although the bass drum has no definite pitch, tune the heads to a very low fundamental tone while still maintaining a warm, round sound. The type of head greatly contributes to the final sound.

Plastic heads are recommended for school use. They have the ability to withstand abuse and still remain functional. Periodically, clean plastic heads with a sponge and warm water. The heads will occasionally have to be removed in order to clean dirt and residue from the flesh-hoop, counter-hoop and shell. If the head appears to be warped or the collar has been stretched beyond the normal amount, it is time for replacement.

Care should be exercised when selecting a new head. For marching use, a thicker head is preferable because of its durability. For concert use, a thinner coated head or a simulated calf head (fiber-skin) will work well. For professional use, nothing can replace the warm tone of a real calf-skin head.

CONCERT BASS DRUM AND STAND

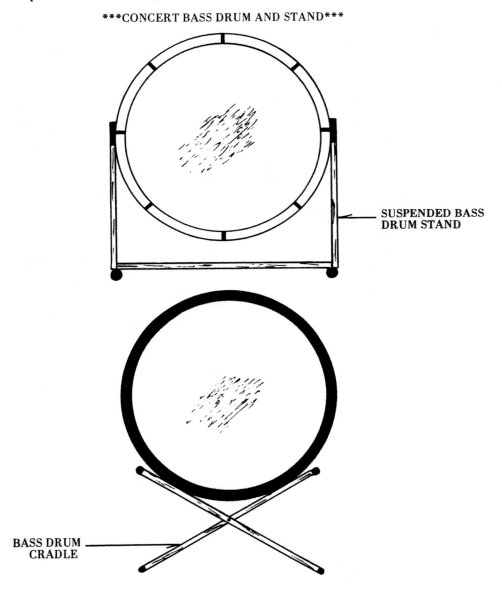

SUSPENDED BASS DRUM STAND

BASS DRUM CRADLE

*** THE CALF–SKIN HEAD ***

Because calf-skin heads are susceptible to change in temperature and humidity, the player must constantly adjust the head tension to properly maintain the sound. It is of utmost importance to tighten the bass drum head when it is not in use. An important rule in caring for a calf-skin head is: MAINTAIN THE HEAD IN THE OPPOSITE CONDITION IT IS USED FOR PERFORMANCE. Since the bass drum head must be loosened to obtain a low, resonant sound, be sure to tighten it when not in use. Maintaining it in this manner will insure enough collar availability to loosen for the low sound. Conversely, the calf head on a snare drum should be stored in a loosened condition. In this way, the collar will not be so stretched that the head cannot be tightened to obtain the crisp sound necessary for snare drum playing.

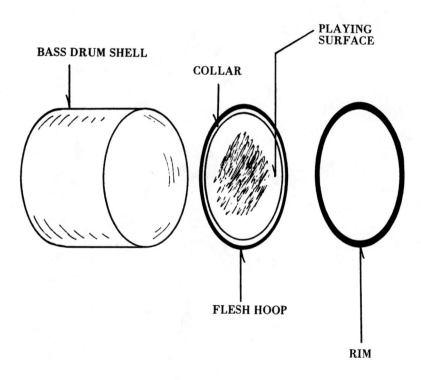

BASS DRUM SHELL

PLAYING SURFACE

COLLAR

FLESH HOOP

RIM

Before the rehearsal or performance, loosen the head of the bass drum to the desired tension for the proper sound. Loosen and tighten the tension evenly by adjusting the lugs in pairs at opposite ends.

Head tension can change between the beginning of a rehearsal and the first entrance. Changes in the weather, the temperature on stage or the hot lights are all causes for the calf head to change.

If the air is dry and the lights are hot, moisture in the heads will evaporate and cause the tension to tighten. The remedy for this is to have a small bowl of water and a sponge on stage. Rub the surface of the head in a circular motion with the damp sponge. This will replace the moisture in the head and the tension on the head will loosen. This process may need to be repeated several times during a rehearsal or performance depending on the stage temperature and humidity.

DO NOT OVERWET HEAD. This will leave it in an unplayable condition.

The opposite problem exists when the humidity is high or it is raining. However, because of the thickness of the head, this rarely puts the bass drum in an unplayable condition as it could with a calf-skin timpani head.

The playing head of the bass drum is tuned slightly tighter than the resonating head, so more articulate patterns may be performed. Also, it may be noted, that a plastic head may be used on the resonating side of the bass drum, while a calf-skin head is on the playing side.

BASS DRUM

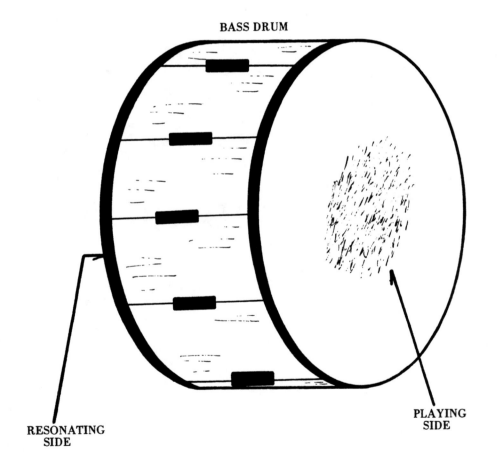

PLAYING
SIDE

RESONATING
SIDE

*** REPAIRING A DAMAGED HEAD ***

If a hole or tear occurs in the head, it should be repaired to avoid buzzing or further damage. If it is small, take a razor blade and carefully trim away the edges of the tear from each other. An unwanted buzz occurs when these two torn edges meet.

Duct tape can be used as a patch by applying it to the hole from the inside of the drum. No harm will occur by leaving the hole open as long as it is not in the playing area of the drum head.

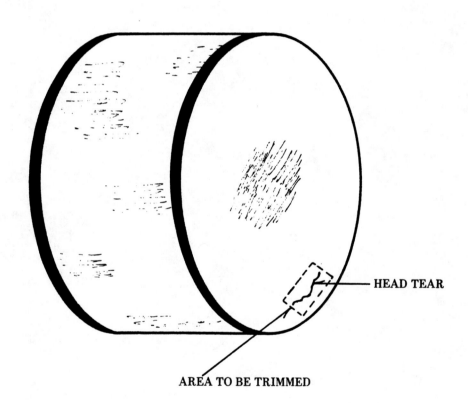

HEAD TEAR

AREA TO BE TRIMMED

*** CORRECTING BASS DRUM RATTLES AND NOISES ***

Before the new head is put on, any rattles or buzzes in the shell should be removed. To accomplish this, first trace the source of the noise and then eliminate it. Tighten all nuts and bolts inside the shell and check for any cracks in the wood shell itself.

Another problem area is the bass drum stand. The standard metal stand is usually guilty of its share of rattles and buzzes.

The first place to check is the angle brace which is located between the two supporting legs. The wing nut attached to the threaded section will work its way loose and vibrate against the stand. To correct this, place a small piece of duct tape over the wing nut. Placing a small piece of felt or a rubber washer between the wing nut and the metal washer will also keep extra noises to a minimum.

Replace the rubber sleeves on the supporting arm of the stand with a felt sleeve. The rubber or plastic sleeve becomes brittle with age and may also cause a buzzing sound.

This type of bass drum stand can also be made of wood. A strip of felt should be mounted on the wood surface where the drum rests.

STANDARD BASS DRUM CRADLE

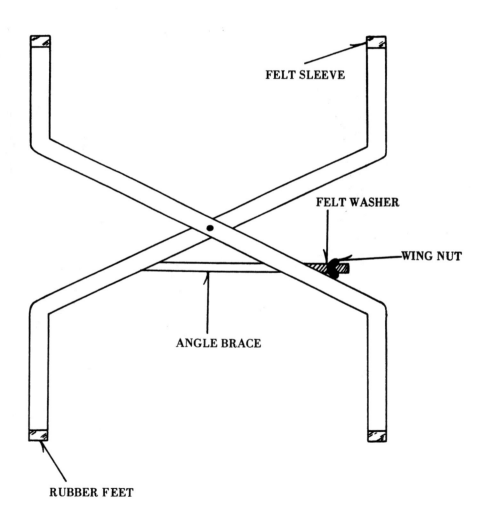

FELT SLEEVE

FELT WASHER

WING NUT

ANGLE BRACE

RUBBER FEET

*** THE SUSPENDED BASS DRUM STAND ***

For a more permanent situation, a suspended stand is best. The drum is totally suspended from elastic sleeves and a hoop which surrounds the drum.

This design is more desirable than the swivel stand with a rod going through the drum, because it allows the bass drum to sound without any restrictions from the stand.

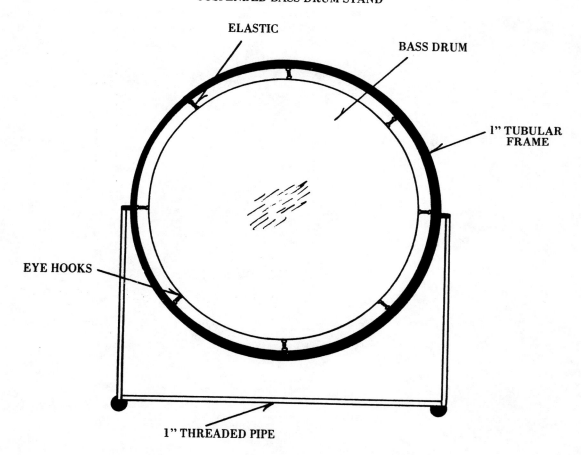

SUSPENDED BASS DRUM STAND

ELASTIC

BASS DRUM

1" TUBULAR FRAME

EYE HOOKS

1" THREADED PIPE

*** REPAIRING THE SHELL ***

A buzz may develop on older drums with a pearl finish because of a separation between the plastic and wood shell. Glue may also become separated from the plastic and create an unwanted sound. The best remedy for this is to remove the pearl finish.

Remove all hardware, including internal mutes and metal manufacturer labels. Carefully peel away the plastic from the wood shell. The plastic covering is easy to remove on older drums because the hardened glue has already virtually separated. If spots are found where the glue is still solidly adhering, and industrial solvent must be used to dissolve it. This process must be done slowly and carefully so as not to harm the drum shell.

Once the pearl has been removed, any remaining glue should be stripped with the solvent. After drying and sanding it lightly, a thin layer of varnish or tung oil should be applied to protect the wood finish.

When replacing the hardware, various precautions can be taken to lessen the possibility of further rattles and buzzes. A small piece of felt can be inserted on the inside of the drum just before the bolt and washer (which holds the lug casing) is attached. This separates the metal from the wood with a soft cushion and reduces sound from the inside of the shell.

A small spring inside the lug casing allows the threaded sleeve, (which is also in the casing) to be exposed and available for the lug. To reduce vibrations between the spring and the casing, wrap a piece of felt or foam rubber around this spring.

LUG CASING

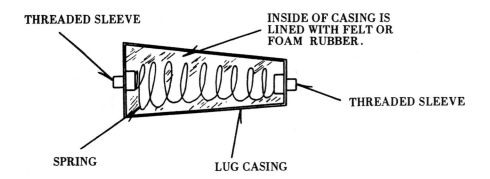

THREADED SLEEVE   INSIDE OF CASING IS LINED WITH FELT OR FOAM RUBBER.

THREADED SLEEVE

SPRING   LUG CASING

*** T- KNOBS ***

T-knobs are made from two metal sections wedged together. Inspect them carefully because if they have become loosened at the point they are wedged together, a rattle may develop. Replace the T-knobs if this has occurred.

A temporary solution would be to wrap the T-knob with duct tape to prevent the two sections from vibrating against each other.

T- KNOB

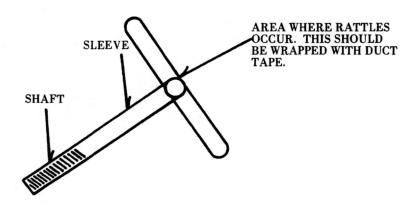

SLEEVE

AREA WHERE RATTLES OCCUR. THIS SHOULD BE WRAPPED WITH DUCT TAPE.

SHAFT

*** CHANGING BASS DRUM HEADS ***

Replace a plastic bass drum head in the following manner:

1. Remove the old head.
2. Thoroughly clean the rim of the shell and then wipe the entire drum clean.
3. Mount the new head evenly over the shell.
4. Replace the counter-hoop over the flesh hoop of the new head.
5. Re-thread each lug evenly and tighten them to the desired tension.

Mounting a calf-skin bass drum head is a more involved process. The following procedures for replacing a calf-skin head are:

1. Clean the shell as before.
2. Moisten the new calf head by wetting a sponge and spreading the water evenly around the head.
3. The edge of the head must be wet enough to form the new collar: however, too much moisture can cause it to separate from the hoop.
4. Evenly seat the head onto the drum.
5. Take the wooden counter-hoop and place it over the flesh hoop of the new head.
6. Replace the lugs and tighten each one by hand until the wrinkles begin to disappear.
7. As the head begins to dry, (usually overnight), periodically re-moisten lightly and increase the tension on the head.

This process takes time but it will insure a good collar on the head which is very important in producing a warm resonant tone. Keeping moisture in the head also prevents it from drying out too fast and possibly splitting.

*** BASS DRUM MUFFLING ***

It is strongly recommended that any muffling of the bass drum, whether internal or external, be used for non-concert performance only. In a concert situation, all muffling should be done by the performer with proper performance techniques. (ie. Either knee, hand or a combination of the two.)

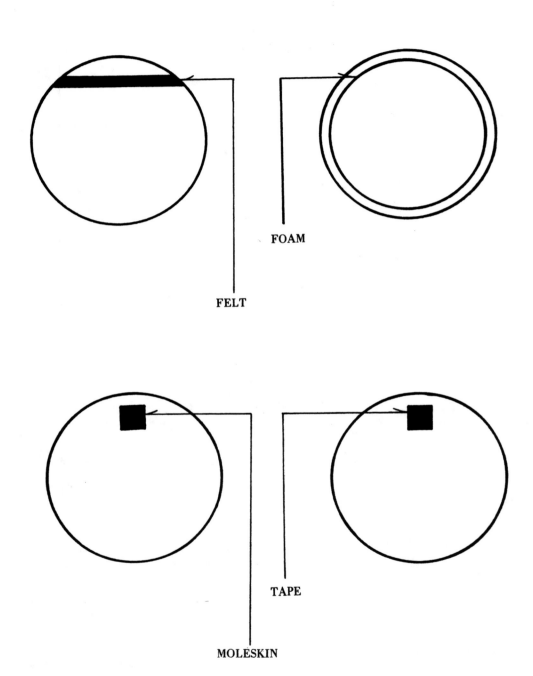

FOAM

FELT

TAPE

MOLESKIN

BASS DRUM-CYMBAL ATTACHMENT

3/8" BOLT AND WINGNUT.
FELT IS PLACED BETWEEN CYMBAL AND
WOOD.

C-CLAMPS(ONE ON EACH SIDE)

1"x4"

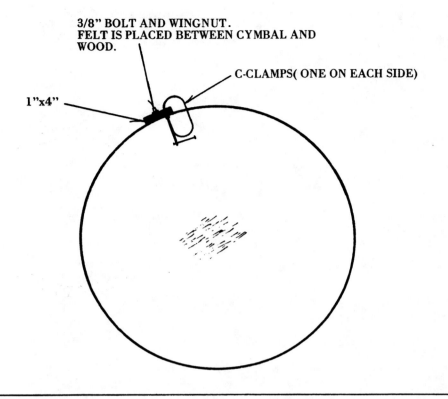

BASS DRUM-CYMBAL ATTACHMENT

CYMBAL   **FOAM RUBBER**

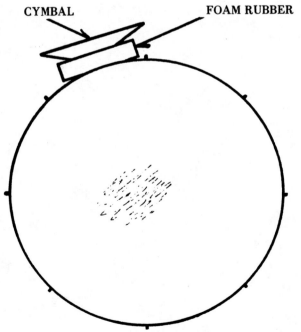

ONLY A LIGHT,SMALL CYMBAL SHOULD BE USED FOR THIS METHOD.

*** SNARE DRUM ***

In order to meet the demands of the percussion literature, the contemporary percussionist in today's highly competitive music business will need to own a number of different snare drums. Some of the different types and combinations of snare drums are as follows:

1. Metal shell drum with plastic heads and wire snares.
2. Metal shell drum with gut snares and calf heads.
3. Wood shell drum with plastic heads and wire snares.
4. A wood shell drum with gut snares and calf heads.
5. Any combination of wood or metal shell with gut or wire snares and calf or plastic heads.
6. There is also the possibility of adding a combination wire/gut snare to the drums above.
7. Snare drums come in sizes ranging from piccolo (3" shell) to military drum (6" shell).

Maintaining the snare drum in good order will keep it working properly and sounding professional.

*** KEEPING THE HEADS CLEAN ***

Periodically, remove plastic heads from the drum and clean any accumulation of dust and dirt. Plastic heads may be cleaned with soapy water. If any irregular shape is noticed after the head is removed, re-place it.

While the head is off, clean the rims and lugs. For metal rims, use steel wool and lightly rub down both the inside and outside of the rim. Wipe clean with a cloth and replace on the drum.

Clean all dirt and grime from the lugs and apply a small amount of vaseline to each one. This will enable the lugs to be threaded and tightened easily.

*** SNARE ADJUSTMENT ***

Snares are in constant need of adjustment. When replacing them, be sure there is equal distance between the rim and the snares on both sides.

SNARE SPACING ACROSS BOTTOM DRUM HEAD

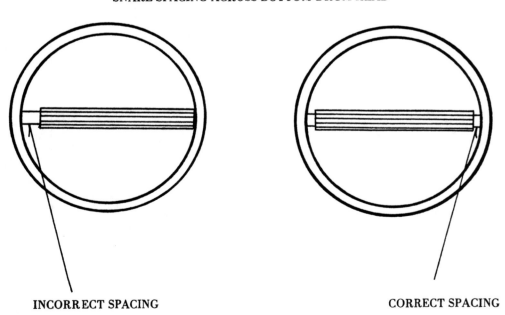

INCORRECT SPACING   CORRECT SPACING

With gut snares, it is important that the snares bend evenly and tightly as they go to the butt end and the strainer. This will insure a tight fit against the bottom head, producing the most sensitive snare sound.

When replacing a set of gut snares, insert a moist piece of paper towel between the snares and drum head at each end as they turn up to the butt end and the strainer.

FITTING GUT SNARES ACROSS BOTTOM DRUM HEAD

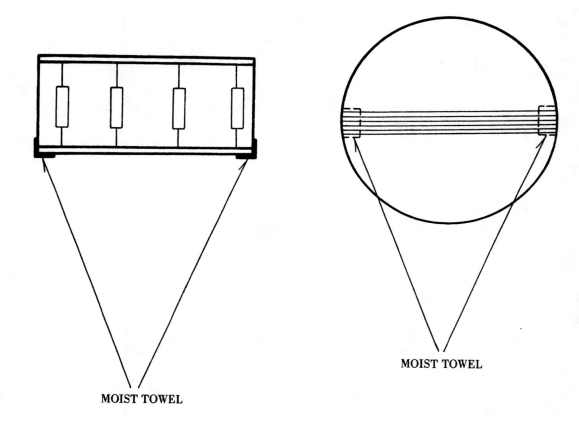

MOIST TOWEL

MOIST TOWEL

THE MOIST PAPER TOWEL HELPS THE NEW GUT SNARE CONFORM TO THE SHAPE OF THE SHELL AS THEY ARE DRYING. WHEN THE SNARES ARE COMPLETELY DRY, REMOVE THE TOWELS.

Finally, the strainer should be checked to be sure it operates with relative ease. Occasionally, the throw-off lever becomes bent into the shell. This will interfere with the working of the strainer and should be adjusted properly.

STRAINER THROW—OFF ADJUSTMENT

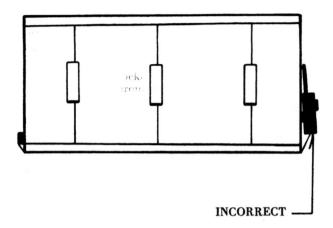

INCORRECT

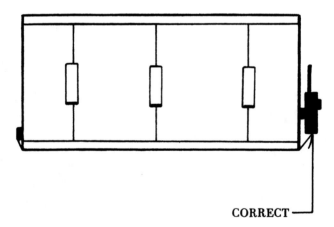

CORRECT

THE STRAINER THROW—OFF SHOULD BE ADJUSTED AWAY FROM THE DRUM SHELL SO THAT IT MAY BE ENGAGED WITH RELATIVE EASE.

A common error in adjusting the strainer is that the snares are pulled too tightly against the head. This will choke the sound of the drum. Just tighten the snares enough to remove any rattling that may occur.

A good performance habit to develop is to turn off the strainer when the drum is not in use. This will avoid any sympathetic vibrations which might cause the snares to rattle during a rehearsal or performance. A wood dowel can be inserted between the snares and the bottom head during long periods of rests, avoiding this problem. Be sure to remove the dowels before the drum is played.

SNARE ISOLATION AWAY FROM HEAD

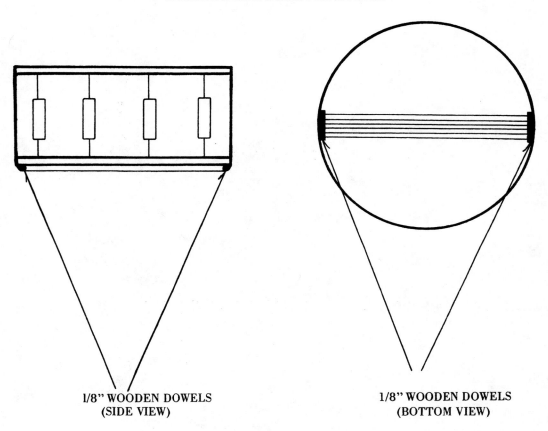

1/8" WOODEN DOWELS
(SIDE VIEW)

1/8" WOODEN DOWELS
(BOTTOM VIEW)

THE WOODEN DOWELS HELP ISOLATE THE SNARES FROM THE HEAD EVENLY, THUS REDUCING THE POSSIBILITY OF UNWANTED NOISE.

When the drum is being stored, it should be left with snares engaged. It is easy to snag the snares if they are loose and hanging from the drum. This is particularly important with gut snares because they will also tend to lose their shape if left in a loosened condition. Consequently, they will not hug the bottom head as well and a certain degree of sensitivity will be lost.

If a wire snare becomes bent, simply remove it with a pair of wire cutters.

*** TUNING THE SNARE DRUM ***

Although the snare drum is not tuned to a specific pitch, there is an element of adjustment necessary to properly tune the snare drum. The pitch or tension on the head is not determined by sound as much as feel. Each player will adjust the drum head to a comfortable tension.

The reason a snare drum cannot be tuned to a specific pitch is because of the resonating chamber. As indicated below, a sound chamber with a curved bowl will produce a clear tone and more definite pitch than a two-headed drum with an open shell.

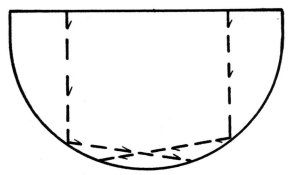

A CURVED REFLECTING SURFACE ALLOWS FOR
A CLEAR TONE AND DEFINITE PITCH PRODUCTION.

THE SOUND PATTERN CAN ONLY TRAVEL
UP AND DOWN WITH THIS SHAPE, THEREFORE
ONLY ALLOWING NON-PITCHED TONE PRODUCTION.

The following are suggestions for maintaining a properly tuned snare drum:

1. Tighten or loosen each lug equally with a one-half turn.
2. The lugs can be adjusted by pairs on opposite sides or in a circular motion around the drum.
3. The snare head should be tighter than the batter head, but this again depends on the players preference.
4. The snares must lie evenly along the bottom head to produce a sensitive snare sound.
5. The strainer must not be so tight that it causes the snares to choke the sound of the drum.
6. Do not muffle the drum with an internal muffler. A certain amount of ring is necessary to give some life to the drum. If an excessive ring exists, control this with a small piece of mole-skin resting on the top head. Also, by loosening one lug on either side of the snares, the ring can be lessened.

SECTIONS OF THE SNARE DRUM

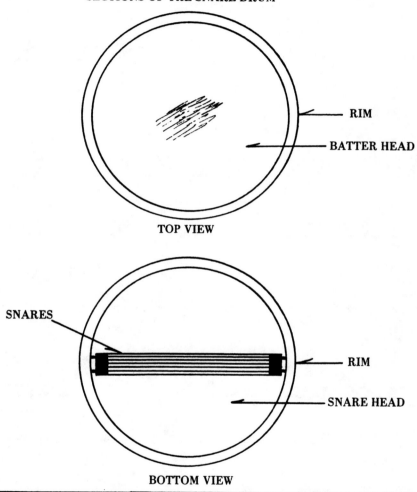

RIM

BATTER HEAD

TOP VIEW

SNARES

RIM

SNARE HEAD

BOTTOM VIEW

INTERNAL MUFFER THROW-OFF

COUNTER-HOOP

THROW-OFF LEVER

SNARE ADJUSTMENT

SNARE STRAINER ADJUSTMENT

HOOP

LUG CASING

BUTT PLATE

AIR HOLE   TENSION ROD

*** TUNING GROUPS OF DRUMS ***

The use of multiple drums in percussion is very common. From the standard drum-set to the complex set-ups in the solo percussion literature, drums of all types are used in combination to form melodic tom-tom parts. Even though the drums are not tuned to specific pitches, they are tuned in intervals relative to each other.

For example, a drum set may be tuned to a chord in thirds with the bass drum as the root of the chord, the tom-toms as the inner notes, and the snare drum as the highest pitch. Smaller toms or roto-toms can also be used to create notes even higher than the snare drum.

The drums can be tuned in a number of ways to obtain different characteristics. For example:

1. Jazz drums have more ring to them and are higher in pitch.
2. A fusion or funk sound would require less ring and more of a dryer quality. The pitch of the drums would also be lower.
3. A concert snare drum is played fairly tight and has a clean, crisp sound.
4. For recording, the drums must be dry with very little ring.

The above are approximate tunings; many variations are possible for every variety of music. The type of head and shell used also affects the sound of the drum. A metal shell will have a brighter sound than a wood shell drum.

TYPICAL DRUM HEAD USE

HEAD THICKNESS		TONE	PITCH	RESPONSE	TENSION
THIN	CLASSICAL/ JAZZ	BRILLIANT	HIGH	QUICK	TIGHT
MED.	GENERAL/ FUSION	MELLOW	MED.	AVERAGE	MEDIUM/ TIGHT
HEAVY	MARCHING	BRILLIANT	HIGH	QUICK	TIGHT
	ROCK/ STUDIO	MED. DARK	LOW	MED. SLOW	MED. LOOSE

DRUM HEAD TENSION

HEAD	TIGHT	MODERATE	LOOSE
PITCH	HIGH	MEDIUM	LOW
SUGGESTED USE	CLASSICAL / JAZZ	GENERAL/ DANCE BAND	STUDIO/ ROCK

*** THE INTERNAL DRUM MUTE ***

An important consideration in using drum mutes is not to overuse them. The internal mute should not be used if it detrimentally affects the sound of the drum. A dry sound may be perfect for recording or funk music; but in a typical concert setting, a certain amount of ring is beneficial. A small amount of ring to a drum helps in projecting the sound. If a drum rings more than is desired, try loosening a lug on either side of the snares before using a mute.

An internal mute should rarely be used because it changes the quality of sound by restricting the vibrating pattern of the drum.

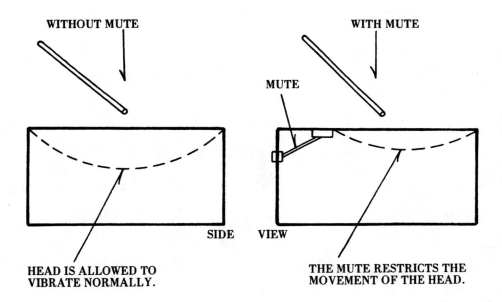

WITHOUT MUTE

WITH MUTE

MUTE

SIDE   VIEW

HEAD IS ALLOWED TO
VIBRATE NORMALLY.

THE MUTE RESTRICTS THE
MOVEMENT OF THE HEAD.

An external mute is preferred if a mute must be used at all. It allows the head to vibrate in a natural manner while still dampening the sound. Also, internal mufflers, when tightened too much, will cause an excessive strain on the head. This will create an uneven sound over the surface of the head and may cause the head to split while playing.

A small piece of moleskin or duct tape will suffice as a drum mute. Below is a very effective homemade mute.

*** EXTERNAL SNARE DRUM MUTE ***

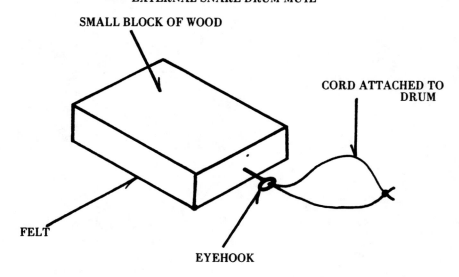

SMALL BLOCK OF WOOD

CORD ATTACHED TO
DRUM

FELT

EYEHOOK

*** REPLACING A SNARE DRUM HEAD ***

Check the old heads for dents, stretching or cuts. If any of these conditions exists, it may be necessary to replace the head.

The following are simple steps for replacing a head on a drum:

1. Remove the old head. Keep all the lugs and washers in a central location to prevent losing them.
2. Clean the rim and inner shell with a piece of steel wool or cloth. Remove any dirt or objects that may have found their way into the shell.
3. Place the new head on the shell and secure the conterhoop over the head.
4. Tighten all lugs by hand until they are secure.
5. Tighten each lug one-half turn with a drum key, either in a circular pattern around the drum or in opposite pairs.
6. As the head is being tightened, a cracking sound will occur; this is merely the glue in the flesh-hoop settling.
7. Press the heel of the hand down on the center of the head periodically as the head is being tightened. This will loosen the head slightly and keep the cracking of the glue to a minimum.
8. Keep one hand on the lug that was first tightened as the rest are being tightened. By doing this your work pattern will remain consistent. This will insure that each lug will have equal tension, creating an even sound on the drum.

MEMBRANE STICK AND MALLET SELECTION

	S.D. STICK	WOOD	HARD FELT	MED. FELT	SOFT FELT	OTHERS
TIMP.	LIGHT UN-PITCHED TONE	PUNCTUATED BRITTLE SOUND REDUCES PITCH	GOOD TONE. WARMER THAN WOOD	LESS NOTE CLARIFICA-TION GENERAL USAGE	BEST FOR SUS-TAINING ROLLS	BRUSHES MARACAS
BASS DRUM	BRITTLE NON-CHARACTERISTIC SOUND	ACCENTED ARTICULATE RHYTHMIC	GOOD FOR FORTE. ACCENTED RHYTHMIC	GOOD FUNDAMEN-TAL SOUND	GOOD FOR ROLLS	RUTE BRUSHES

	S.D. STICK	DOWELS	YARN	CORD	TIMP. MALLET	BRUSHES
SNARE DRUM	BEST SOUND	LIGHT ARTICULATE	*	*	*	SUSTAINED SOUND. LESS DEFINITION
TENOR DRUM	ARTICULATE SOUND	,,	*	*	*	,,
TOM-TOMS	,,	,,	NON ARTICULATE GOOD FUNDAMENTAL SOUND	GOOD FOR ROLLS	WARM SOUND GOOD FOR ROLLS	,,
ROTO-TOMS	,,	,,	,,	,,	,,	,,

*These would not normally be used as they do not produce a sound characteristic of the instrument.

NOTE: Congos and Bongos may be played with wooden dowels. This increases volume, but some of their characteristic sound is lost.

✳✳✳ CYMBALS ✳✳✳

Cymbals are standard equipment for the working percussionist. There are very few works in the percussion literature that do not require the use of cymbals. From crash cymbals to suspended, hi-hats to sizzle, antique to finger cymbals — all are an important part of the percussionist's trade.

CYMBAL SET-UPS

HAND CYMBALS

SUSPENDED CYMBAL

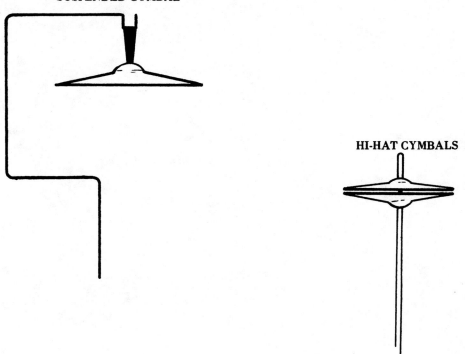

HI-HAT CYMBALS

CROTALES

*** STORAGE OF CYMBALS ***

Because of their construction, cymbals appear to be able to withstand much abuse. In reality, cymbals are fairly delicate instruments requiring special care and handling. To preserve their life and tone, a secure method of storage is recommended. A fiber case with a foam-rubber lining provides excellent protection. The edges of the cymbal are the most vulnerable to damage.

A padded cloth or leather bag also provide adequate protection. One problem with the cloth bags is that the edges of the cymbals tend to cut through the bottom when the bag is placed down.

Cymbal slots in trap cases are also excellent storage areas; they should be lined with foam, especially on the bottom.

Avoid leaving cymbals on the floor or leaning against other objects where they could be stepped on and damaged. Ideally, the best storage is to have the cymbals lying flat with a thin layer of felt in between.

*** METHODS OF CYMBAL STORAGE ***

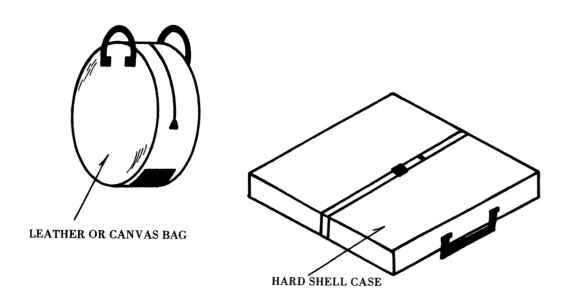

LEATHER OR CANVAS BAG

HARD SHELL CASE

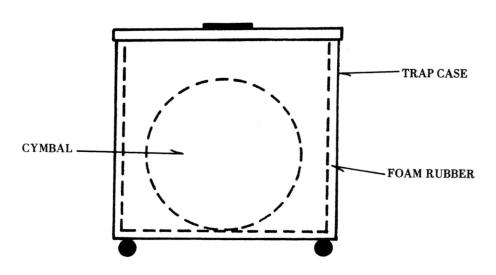

TRAP CASE

CYMBAL

FOAM RUBBER

*** REPAIRING A CRACKED CYMBAL ***

As careful as a cymbal player might be, there is always the possibility of developing a crack. A crack generally occurs from misuse or accident. Possibly a cymbal is too light for the necessary volume needed and overplaying may result. If a cymbal is dropped and a slight dent in the edge occurs, the cymbal will eventually tend to crack at this point.

Once a crack develops, it must be eliminated or the cymbal cannot be used.

There are three main areas where cracks can occur: the bell, the body and the edge.

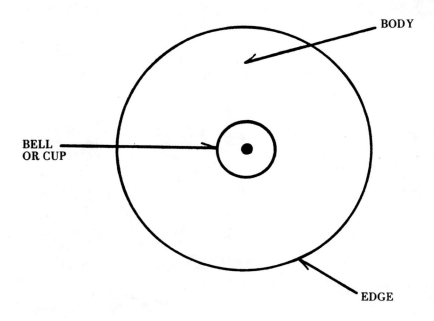

A crack at the bell or cup may be the result of not using a protective sleeve on a stand. This sleeve, which can be made of rubber or leather, keeps the metal of the cymbal from having direct contact with the threaded portion of the stand.

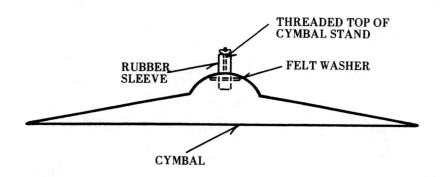

The procedure for repairing a crack in the bell or body is as follows:

1. Using a small center-punch, mark a spot at each extreme edge of the crack on the underside of the cymbal.
2. Drill a hole approximately 1/8" at these two points.
3. Continue drilling holes every 1/4" along the actual crack.
4. Using a small round file, connect the holes with a circular (twisting) motion. Do not file in an up-and-down motion, as this will put stress on the metal.
5. Lightly sand the edge of both sides of the cut to remove any sharp burrs.

When selecting the original endpoints of the crack, be sure to include the entire crack. If any part of it is not removed, additional cracking will result. When drilling, it is important to brace the bottom of the cymbal with a block of wood. This keeps the drill bit from splitting the cymbal.

DRILLING OUT A CYMBAL CRACK

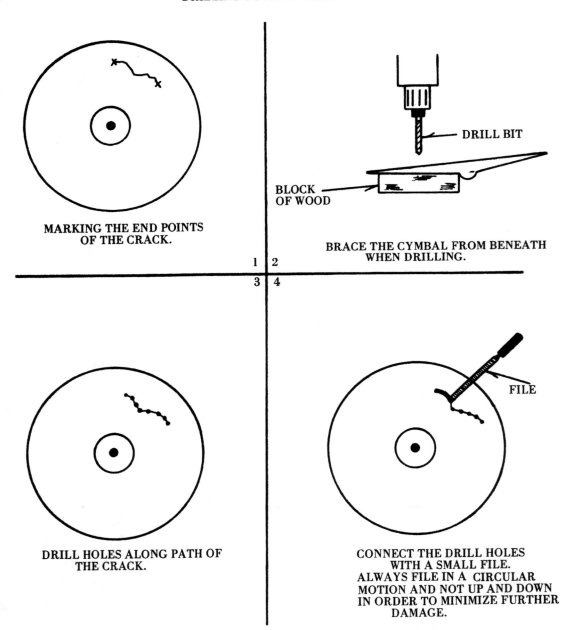

MARKING THE END POINTS
OF THE CRACK.

BRACE THE CYMBAL FROM BENEATH
WHEN DRILLING.

DRILL HOLES ALONG PATH OF
THE CRACK.

CONNECT THE DRILL HOLES
WITH A SMALL FILE.
ALWAYS FILE IN A CIRCULAR
MOTION AND NOT UP AND DOWN
IN ORDER TO MINIMIZE FURTHER
DAMAGE.

If a crack is more developed than a single split (spider-webbing), a larger portion of the cymbal will have to be removed. Trace the outer parameter of the cracks from its end points with a series of holes, so it completely surrounds the damaged area. Then remove the entire cracked portion of the cymbal as explained previously.

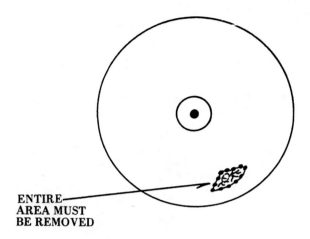

ENTIRE
AREA MUST
BE REMOVED

The edge of the cymbal is the most common area to be damaged. It is very susceptible to damage from dropping or striking other objects. At first, the damage appears as a dent; this may eventually become the beginning of a crack. From constant playing, vibrations focus on the dented area causing the metal to crack. As in previous cases, the crack must be removed.

There are two basic methods for removing the cracked area. A single crack in a small area may be removed by taking a pie-shaped portion out of the cymbal. The pie cut surrounds the damaged area by removing a one-inch section on either side of the crack.

If the damage consists of several spider-webbed areas, it may be eliminated either by drilling and filing as before, or it may be sawed with a band saw. When sawing, take the same precautions as when drilling; keep the cymbal flat against the table. Proceed slowly and carefully. Remove all sharp burrs caused by the saw blade.

Taking such a large section from the cymbal weakens its overall strength; however, it lessens the possibility of the crack reappearing and allows the cymbal to be used.

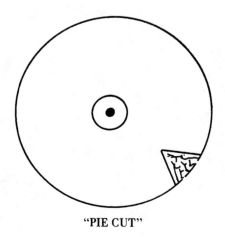

"PIE CUT"

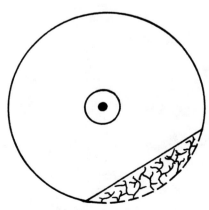

LARGE AREA REMOVAL
BY BAND SAW

*** WELDING A CRACK ***

Some success has been obtained by making a small weld if the crack is at the edge of the cymbal. This is particularly useful for marching cymbals; for example, where a great amount of force and volume are need - ed and the removal of a section of the cymbal would reduce its strength.

A high-grade silver solder can be used to connect the two cracked edges. The solder must be heated to a high temperature (1100 to 1400 degrees). This will produce a very hard weld that can withstand a great amount of pressure. The problem in using high heat to fuse a crack is the possibility of diminished tonal quality. Since the cymbal had already been tempered in its original production, reheating it may produce a change in the tonal quality. However, marching cymbals utilize much more volume than tone so this is not a crucial point. Welding should be used only in extreme cases and only on a heavy cymbal. The high temperature may melt a very thin cymbal.

Warping may also result if the hot cymbal comes in contact with water. To prevent this, allow the cymbal to gradually cool. Residue from the weld can be removed by buffing it lightly on a wheel.

Regardless of the method used for repairing a cymbal, there is no guarantee this will be the end of the damage. The crack may begin again at some future time. Also, since the cymbal was meant to be played with the entire surface intact, removal of any metal will affect its overall tone. However, repairing the cymbal does extend its overall life, and much success has been had in repairing cymbals.

*** CLEANING AND POLISHING CYMBALS ***

The question of how much to clean cymbals depends on the individual. Some performers feel that keeping the cymbals clean periodically with a cleansing agent preserves the bright sound and high overtones. Other players voice the opinion that the dirt in the grooves helps in the aging process and cultivates the dark sound that has less overtones.

Whether a cleansing agent is used or not, the following are suggestions for the care of your cymbals.

1. Handle the cymbals by the edge just as you would a phonograph record. This eliminates finger-prints which attract dust.
2. Periodically, dust off the cymbals to prevent an unnecessarily thick build-up of dirt.
3. If a cleansing agent is to be used, several commercial cymbal cleaners are available.
4. Do not use steel wool pads or brass cleaner on the cymbals, as they contain abrasives that can scar the finish.
5. Rub the cleaner with the grain of the cymbal in a circular motion. This helps in removing deeply imbedded dirt.
6. Remove all traces of the cleaner from the cymbal. If any is left, it will attract more residue, causing additional cleaning.
7. Keep the cymbals covered when not in use and wipe them off after each use, keeping the finish free from dust and oil.

The addition of rivets create and added level of sound for the performer. Composers write for sizzle cymbals, and drum-set players creatively use this sound in their improvisation.

When the cymbal is struck, the rivets continue to vibrate against the body of the cymbal causing a longer, sustained sound; This sound is quite different from the normal cymbal. Thin cymbals work best as sizzle cymbals. A cymbal can be bought with the rivets already attached or they can be added.

The procedure for attaching rivets to a suspended cymbal is as follows:

1. Lightly mark each spot with a center punch on the underside of the cymbal where the rivets are to be placed.
2. As few as two or as many as eight rivets can be added.
3. Always brace the cymbal from underneath with a block of wood before drilling.
4. Stagger the rivets slightly on the surface of the cymbal. If all the rivets are placed along the same groove, the cymbal will be weakened.
5. Rivets can be brass or ordinary metal. Brass rivets are recommended because they react quickly and sustain longer.
6. Once the rivets are inserted, slightly bend them at the bottom to prevent them from coming out of the hole.
7. The rivets should be able to move freely within the hole; therefore, the holes need to be slightly larger than the rivet.

A sizzle cymbal can be improvised on the spot with a coin and a piece of tape. Place the tape half-way across the coin and then connect it to the body of the cymbal. When the cymbal is struck, the vibrations will cause the coin to vibrate in the same manner as the rivets.

SIZZLE CYMBALS

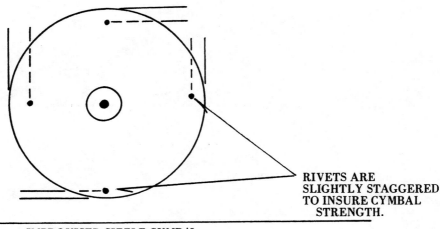

RIVETS ARE
SLIGHTLY STAGGERED
TO INSURE CYMBAL
STRENGTH.

IMPROVISED SIZZLE CYMBAL

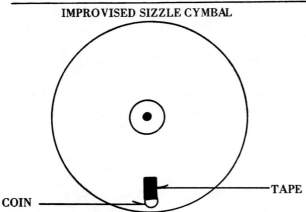

COIN ————— TAPE

*** SUSPENDED CYMBAL ***

The ideal method of suspending a cymbal is with a crook or boom stand. There are many advantages to this type of suspension as opposed to the traditional suspended cymbal stand.

1. Because the cymbal hangs freely and is not constricted by the wing nut attachment, tone is improved.
2. There is a greater reduction in stand noise with this type of suspension.
3. With the boom stand, there is additional flexibility in placing the cymbal within a multiple percussion set-up.
4. Since the strap is attached, the cymbal can be quickly removed and replaced with a different size during the course of a work.
5. The cymbal can also be quickly removed if it is one of a pair and used as crash cymbals.

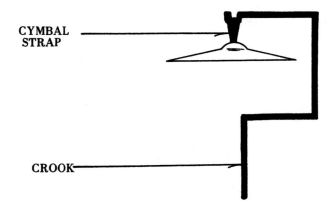

CYMBAL STRAP

CROOK

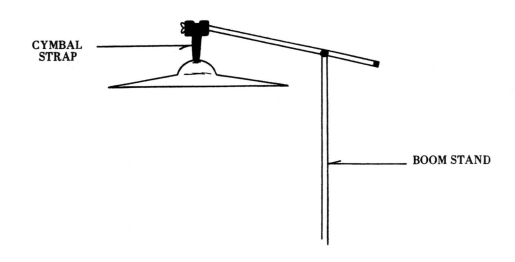

CYMBAL STRAP

BOOM STAND

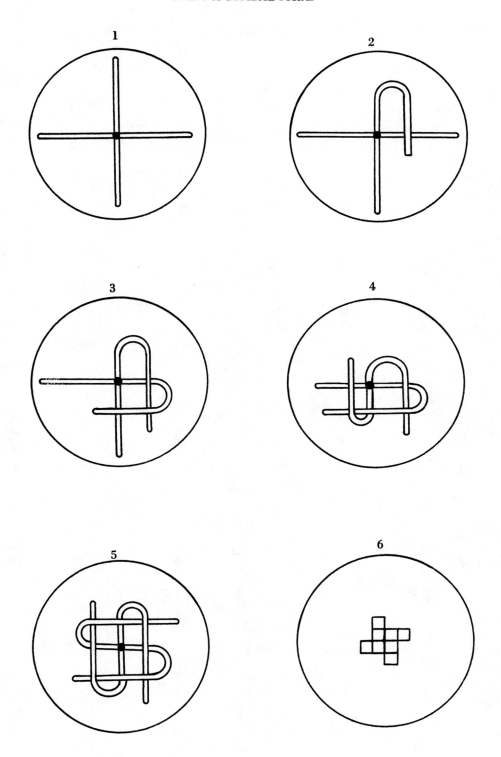

INSIDE VIEW OF CYMBAL

CYMBAL TREE STAND

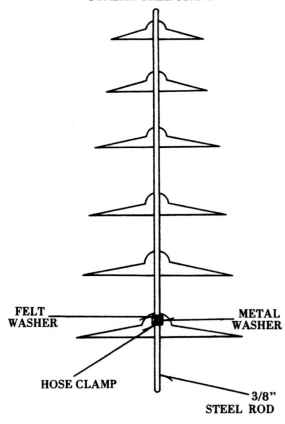

FELT WASHER

METAL WASHER

HOSE CLAMP

3/8" STEEL ROD

CYMBAL BOOM STAND

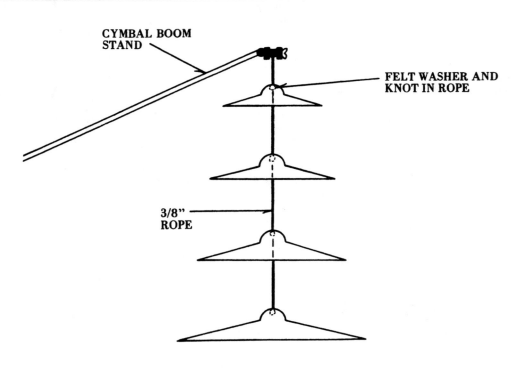

FELT WASHER AND KNOT IN ROPE

3/8" ROPE

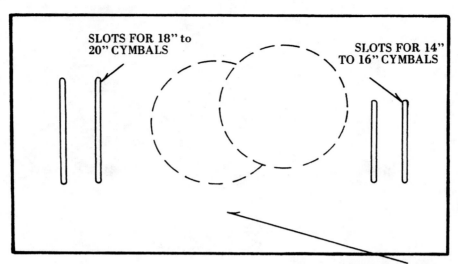

TOP VIEW

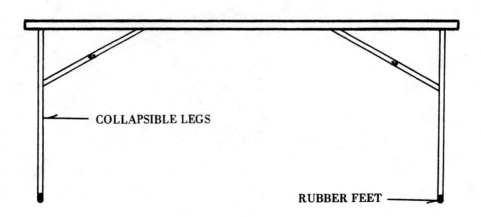

SIDE VIEW

*** FINGER CYMBALS ***

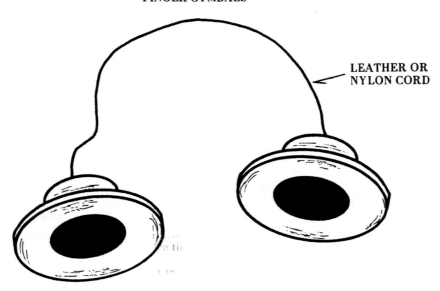

LEATHER OR
NYLON CORD

FINGER CYMBALS SHOULD BE ATTACHED TOGETHER WITH A LEATHER OR NYLON CORD. THIS AIDS IN CONTROLLING THE INSTRUMENT, AND PREVENTS DROPPING THEM DURING PERFORMANCE.

*** CYMBAL RAKE ***

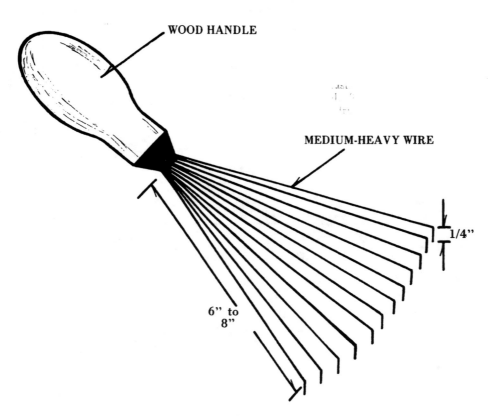

WOOD HANDLE

MEDIUM-HEAVY WIRE

1/4"

6" to
8"

THIS IS MORE EFFECTIVE AS A BRUSH SUBSTITUTE TO CUT THROUGH HEAVY ORCHESTRATIONS.

*** GONGS AND TAM TAMS ***

Composers use both words, "gong" and "tam tam", in the orchestral literature to refer to the large instrument. A more technically accurate description would be to refer to the tam tam as the large instrument and the gong as the smaller, sometimes pitched instrument.

Either one can be damaged by misuse or over-playing. Repairing a gong or tam tam is accomplished in the same manner as with cymbals. Follow the instructions for repairing a crack or split in the metal.

Besides the actual gong or tam tam, the stand and beater are two very important parts of this instrument.

The stand must be strong enough to support the heavy weight of the tam tam and also withstand the back-and-forth motion of the swinging gong after it is struck. The ideal stand supports the instrument with a circular metal ring on a single base. This stand takes a minimum amount of room on stage and can be transported easily with a small dolly.

A gong beater must be of sufficient weight and mass to set the entire instrument in motion as quickly as possible. If the beater is too light, the instrument will tend to speak late. A heavy beater is also necessary to produce the low, fundamental sound of the tam tam.

CIRCULAR GONG/TAM-TAM STAND

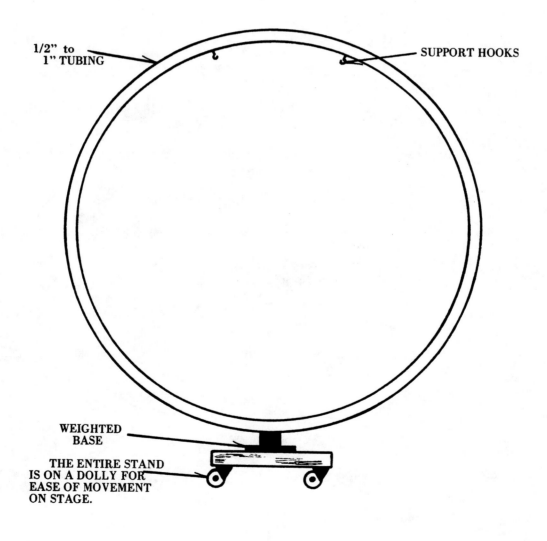

1/2" to 1" TUBING — SUPPORT HOOKS

WEIGHTED BASE

THE ENTIRE STAND IS ON A DOLLY FOR EASE OF MOVEMENT ON STAGE.

GONG STAND

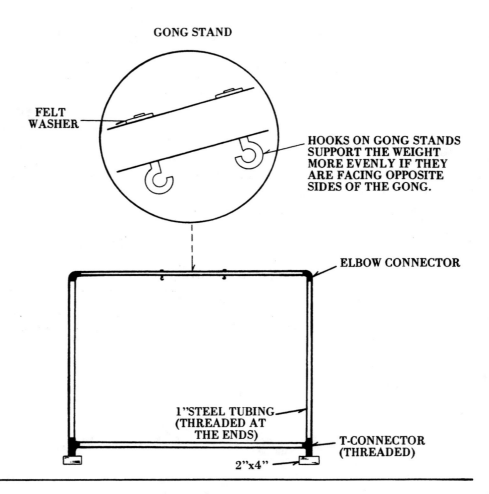

FELT
WASHER

HOOKS ON GONG STANDS
SUPPORT THE WEIGHT
MORE EVENLY IF THEY
ARE FACING OPPOSITE
SIDES OF THE GONG.

ELBOW CONNECTOR

1"STEEL TUBING
(THREADED AT
THE ENDS)

T-CONNECTOR
(THREADED)

2"x4"

*** SUSPENDING THE TAM-TAM ***

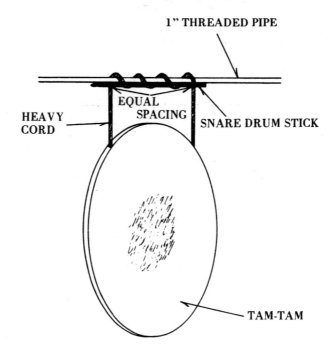

1" THREADED PIPE

EQUAL
SPACING

HEAVY
CORD

SNARE DRUM STICK

TAM-TAM

*** TAMBOURINE ***

The tambourine is frequently used in percussion literature and is an essential part of every percussionist's equipment. It's main parts are the shell, head and jingles. Keeping each of these parts in good condition is important for the proper sound.

*** THE SHELL ***

Although some tambourine shells are constructed of metal and fiberglass, most shells are made of 3/8" wood. The wood shell is the easiest to repair. Most damage to a tambourine shell occurs from dropping or from years of hard playing.

If a crack results from an accident or misuse, it can be restored with glue. Wood glue or epoxy work well.

The following procedure is for repairing a crack in the tambourine shell.

1.   Open the cracked sections slightly with a knife.
2.   Force the glue down the crack as far as possible.
3.   Bring the two sections together as evenly as possible, carefully wiping off excess glue and keeping it away from the jingles and head.
4.   Place a small block of wood on either side of the crack and secure with a C-clamp.
5.   Tighten the clamp slowly until the crack is closed. Do not overtighten or further damage may result.

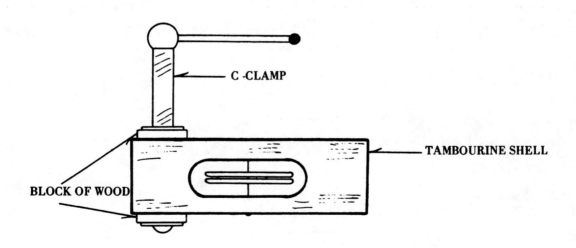

*** JINGLES ***

Jingles are a very important part of the tambourine sound. Occasionally, one will crack or split and eventually fall off. A few missing jingles will not affect the overall sound.

There are many types of metals used in making jingles. German silver is most commonly used. If some of the jingles need replacing, try to use the same type of jingle.

When the tambourine is not in use, keep it wrapped in a bag or towel which will protect both the jingles and head.

*** REPLACING THE HEAD OF A TAMBOURINE ***

As with any drum head, the head of the tambourine is vulnerable to damage. Most tambourine heads are made from calf or goat skin and are by far the most desirable. Plastic-head tambourines are available but are not recommended. Tunable tambourines are also available, but not recommended because of the added weight.

The following procedures are for replacing a tambourine head. Careful preparation is necessary, and each step should be done properly, insuring a satisfactory result. Since certain equipment is needed, be sure to read all instructions before attempting to replace the head.

1. First, remove all of the torn head from the shell, including the section glued to the outer lip. Also, remove all tacks. Try not to destroy any wood on the shell when removing the glued portion of the head.
2. Lightly sand the rim of the shell, removing all traces of old glue.
3. The new calf or goat skin head should be fairly thick and at least two inches larger than the diameter of the shell. Soak the new head in cool water for a few minutes until it becomes pliable. DO NOT use warm or hot water as it tends to shrink the head.
4. While the head is soaking, apply a light layer of white glue to the top rim and the top, outer edge of the shell. Smooth out the glue and remove any excess with your fingers. Remember to keep the glue from getting on the jingles.
5. Remove the head from the water and place it on a towel. Lightly dry the head with the towel, removing water.
6. A clamp is needed to keep tension on the head as it dries. A thick rubber band or a large hose clamp will work; however, the best option is an embroidery hoop. They are available in many sizes. The 10" tambourine is the most popular, so acquire a 10" embroidery hoop.
   The hoops can be made out of plastic, wood or metal. Plastic works best because it does not absorb moisture as the head is drying; a wooden hoop will. The embroidery hoop also has a tension adjustment which can be adjusted while the head is drying.
7. Now the head can be placed evenly on the shell. The overlapping portion of the head should be evenly spaced around the shell.

*** MOUNTING THE TAMBOURINE HEAD ***

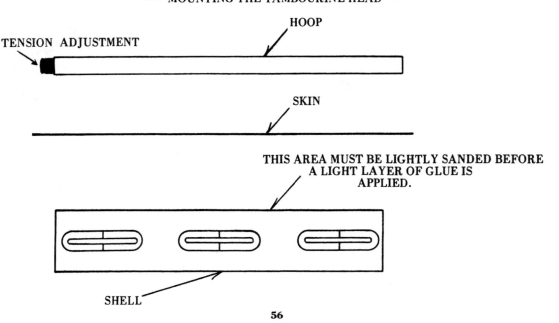

TENSION ADJUSTMENT

HOOP

SKIN

THIS AREA MUST BE LIGHTLY SANDED BEFORE A LIGHT LAYER OF GLUE IS APPLIED.

SHELL

8. Place the hoop over the outer edge of the shell and adjust the tension a moderate amount.
9. As the hoop is pushed down over the head, the tension will tighten. When the hoop is flush with the top of the shell, fully adjust the tension and allow it to dry overnight at room temperature.
10. Periodic moistening of the head with a damp sponge keeps the head from drying too fast.
11. After the head and glue have dried, trim the excess calf with a razor blade. Approximately 3/8" to 1/4" should remain glued to the outer shell as a collar.

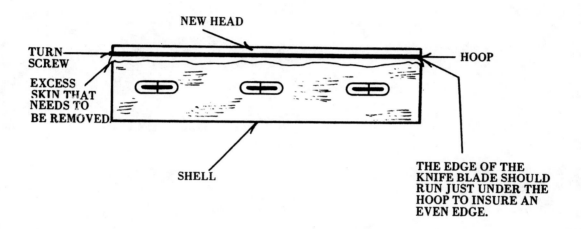

12. The embroidery hoop may now be removed and the tacks replaced. Space the tacks 1 1/2" apart.
13. Finally, apply a thin layer of glue to the inside rim of the head.

The tambourine is now ready for use. Break it in gradually.

On tambourines with shells that are not perfectly round, use two 8" hose clamps attached together. Because there is an adjustment screw on both sides of the hoop, it can be tailored to the exact shape of the shell.

*** THUMB ROLLS ***

There are three solutions to help in preparing the tambourine for thumb rolls. On a head that has a rough surface, no preparation is necessary. For those tambourines with a smoother surface, one of the following solutions may be tried:

1. Rub the edge of the tambourine head with the same rosin violinists use on their bows. This increases the friction of the head and the thumb will work easily.
2. Spray a small strip of tact spray along the edge of the tambourine head to increase the friction.
3. Glue a strip of fine grit sand paper to the edge of the head. This prepares a permanent surface for secure thumb rolls.

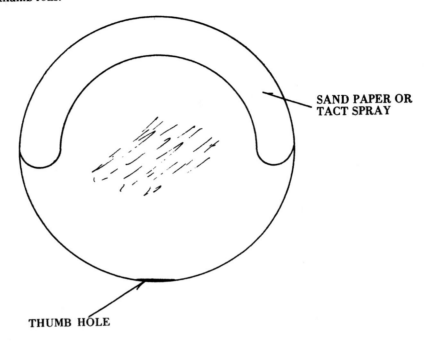

SAND PAPER OR
TACT SPRAY

THUMB HOLE

The age-old tradition of moistening the thumb with saliva before each thumb roll will also help with any solution, but especially when the head has not been altered.

*** TAMBOURINE HOLDER ***

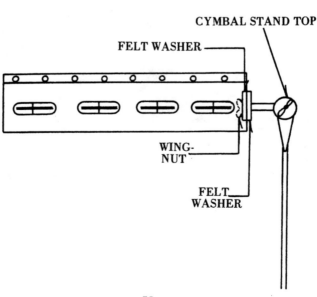

CYMBAL STAND TOP

FELT WASHER

WING-
NUT

FELT
WASHER

*** TRIANGLE ***

TRIANGLE AND CLIP

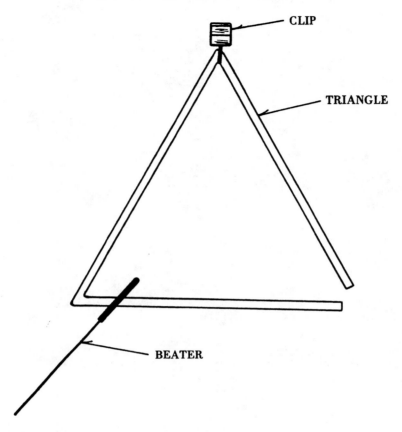

There is very little to repair or maintain on the triangle. Except for some occasional flaking of the chrome plating, which may be caused by over-playing, the triangle is virtually damage free.

The following are some suggestions in selecting and using the triangle:

1. Although any size triangle will work for symphonic music, 6 inches is the standard size. However, the most important factor is the sound of the instrument.
2. Since the presence of overtones helps project the sound and adds beauty to the quality, acquire a triangle with many overtones.
3. Every triangle has an area that sounds best. Experiment with yours to find the area producing the most beautiful sound.
4. Since triangles come in different sizes, be creative and choose the appropriate size for the situation. The standard 6" triangle will be satisfactory for most literature. Larger triangles with a deeper quality sound good for Mahler and Wagner, while certain very soft notes sound excellent on a very small triangle.
5. Dynamics will determine the size of the triangle and beaters.
6. It is very easy to overplay the triangle. Focus on the quality of sound more than volume.
7. The percussionist will have a selection of beaters in different sizes and weight as part of his equipment. Match the beaters in pairs for two-handed playing. Insulate the end of the beater (that is held) with rubber tubing, insuring a solid grip and avoiding dampening of the sound.
8. Do not drop the triangle. To protect the tonal life of the instrument, store it in a cloth bag.

Two very interesting and effective performance techniques on the triangle are vibrato and bending the pitch.

1. To accomplish a vibrato, rapidly move the outer two fingers of the hand holding the clip, in a back and forth motion.
2. Raise the pitch by striking the instrument and then slowly dipping it into a container of water.

*** THE TRIANGLE CLIP ***

WOODEN TRIANGLE CLIP WITH SAFETY STRING

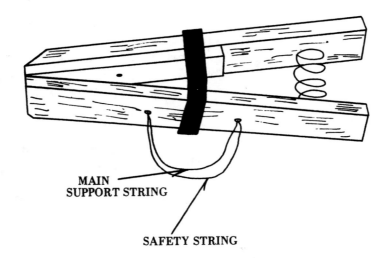

MAIN
SUPPORT STRING

SAFETY STRING

A proper triangle clip is crucial to the sound of the instrument. The material used to suspend the triangle from the clip is directly related to the quality and sustaining power of the instrument. Do not use string, yarn or cord. Gut string or plastic fishing line are ideal.

A welder's clamp is the standard clip available commercially. The spring is very strong and secure. If bought commercially, be sure to replace the suspending string with gut or fishing line. These metal clips should have rubber sleeves at the end to eliminate any sound when the clamp is attached to a metal stand.

METAL TRIANGLE CLIP WITH SAFETY STRING

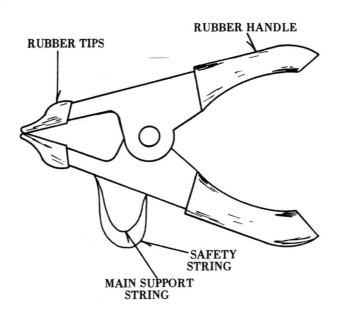

RUBBER HANDLE

RUBBER TIPS

SAFETY
STRING

MAIN SUPPORT
STRING

The loop on the triangle clip should not be too long. If it hangs much below the thickness of the triangle, there will be too much movement of the instrument during loud passages. Also, do not tie it too tightly, or it will choke the sound. A distance of approximately 1/8 inch between the bottom of the clip and the top of the triangle is best for both control and sound. A second string is used as a "safety" in the event the main string breaks during a performance. The second string should be slightly larger than the main one.

*** THE TRIANGLE STAND ***

The use of a triangle stand in orchestral percussion work has many advantages.

1. It allows a greater choice in placing the triangle within the many different percussion set-ups.
2. It avoids the need to clip the triangle to the music stand.
3. The triangle can be raised where the sound can project and not be buried under the music stand.
4. The visual effect of two-beater playing is also enhanced.

The triangle stand is only necessary when two beaters are used or within a multiple set-up when it is not possible to hold the triangle.

TRIANGLE STAND

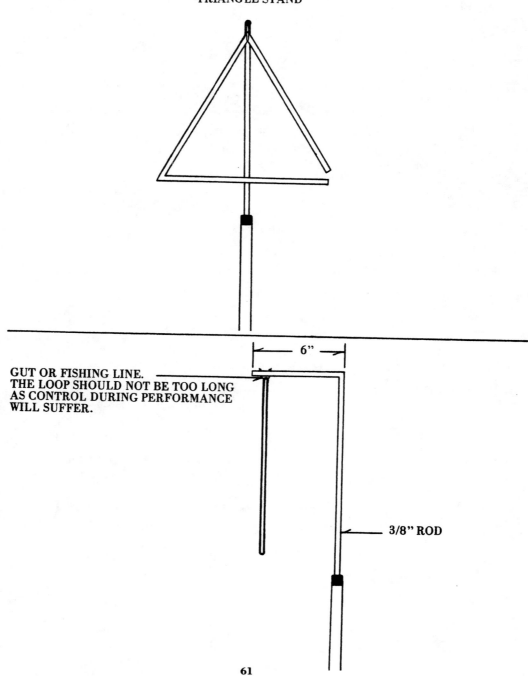

GUT OR FISHING LINE.
THE LOOP SHOULD NOT BE TOO LONG
AS CONTROL DURING PERFORMANCE
WILL SUFFER.

← 6" →

3/8" ROD

*** CROTALES ***

The final instrument in this section on metal percussion instruments is the crotales or antique cymbals. The crotales are ususally suspended by leather thongs or a thick cord for individual use.

CROTALE

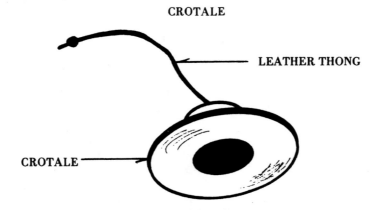

LEATHER THONG

CROTALE

When an entire chromatic set is needed, they should be mounted on a chromatic stand which is available commercially.

COMMERCIALLY AVAILABLE CROTALE STAND

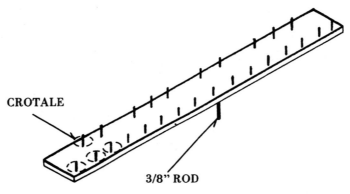

CROTALE

3/8" ROD

If crotales are not available, it is possible to obtain a similar sound by suspending the proper bar from a set of bells and striking it with a heavy finger cymbal.

Below is a sketch of a smaller stand that will hold two crotales. It is very useful in orchestral works such as "Les Noces" and "The Rite of Spring" by Stravinsky, and "Afternoon of a Faun" by Debussy.

DUO—CROTALE STAND

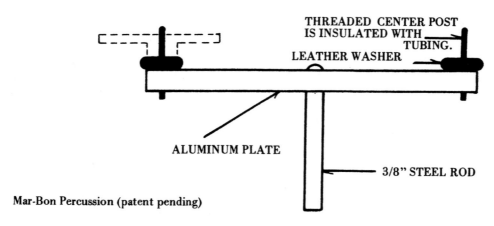

THREADED CENTER POST IS INSULATED WITH TUBING.

LEATHER WASHER

ALUMINUM PLATE

3/8" STEEL ROD

Mar-Bon Percussion (patent pending)

*** ACCESSORY PERCUSSION INSTRUMENTS ***

Being a percussionist is analogous to being a collector of instruments. Our tools are so varied and diverse, we literally collect and build instruments as long as we are in this profession.

A good rule of thumb is to buy the highest quality instruments available. A poor instrument or stand causes more trouble than the money that was saved.

Listed below are some standard accessory percussion instruments and tips on their repair and maintenance.

*** CLAVE ***

Claves are meant to be struck by one another. Using material harder than wood to strike a clave can result in its splintering or developing a crack. Handle any damage of this type in the same manner as a wooden xylophone or marimba bar. Refer to that section for instructions.

*** WOOD BLOCK ***

The woodblock, because of its construction, tends to crack more easily than other wooden bars or instruments. For most compositions, a medium-hard rubber mallet produces the most desirable sound. A snare drum stick can also be used for some works.

As with any wooden instrument, periodically rub it down with a rubbing oil to prevent it from drying out.

*** MARACAS ***

Maracas are also a very delicate instrument. The wooden shell can crack simply from dropping. If this happens, replace the beads and glue the cracked area together.

Maracas are also made with a plastic shell. Although the sound is not quite the same, some chambers are able to be opened by removing the staples from the end of the handle and inserting various beads to produce a different tone color. Some choices would be: dried beans, peas, rice, small seeds, or washers.

***TEMPLE BLOCKS ***

The playing surface of temple blocks occasionally becomes splintered from misuse or overuse. Avoid hitting the blocks with wooden sticks. Hard core yarn or rubber mallets are ideal.

If splintering occurs, sand the rough sections smooth and apply wood putty to the surface. Gradually build up the top of the block to conform to its natural shape and sand it smooth. It can now be painted. Apply several coats of lacquer to seal the wood after painting.

If a large section of wood needs to be replaced, a block of pine or rosewood can be used. Sand the top of the damaged block flat so the new section of wood can be securely glued to it. After cementing the wood to the surface of the block, shape the new section to conform to the original block with a wood rasp. Paint and finish the block in the same manner as before.

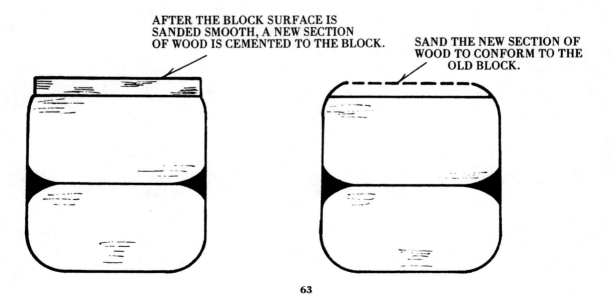

AFTER THE BLOCK SURFACE IS SANDED SMOOTH, A NEW SECTION OF WOOD IS CEMENTED TO THE BLOCK.

SAND THE NEW SECTION OF WOOD TO CONFORM TO THE OLD BLOCK.

It is not uncommon for cracks to develop in temple blocks, expecially to those made from butcher block material. That is, many small sections of wood glued together instead of one solid carved piece. In either case, isolate the cracked sections with a saw. Wood putty can be used to fill in the sawed section; however, this is not recommended because the putty will dry out and tend to vibrate. Leaving a space between the wood sections works best.

*** TEMPLE BLOCK REPAIR ***

A CRACK SOMETIMES DEVELOPS FROM
DROPPING OR OVERPLAYING.

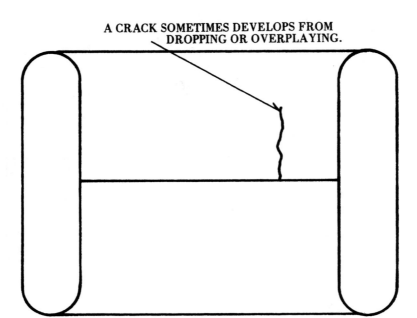

THESE TWO SECTIONS ARE SEPARATED BY SAWING.

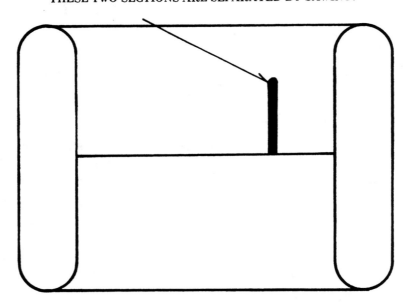

*** WHISTLES AND SIRENS ***

Slide whistles need to be checked for air leaks, especially at the bottom plug. If an air leak develops, use rubber cement or petroleum jelly for repair.

Sirens have a spinning disc within the mouthpiece which creates the sound. After long periods of non-use, this area may need a bit of oil, thereby allowing it to spin freely.

Generally, all mouthpieces need to be cleaned periodically with soap and water.

*** RATCHET ***

The tongues (which make contact with the revolving gear to produce the sound) are a prime area of concern with ratchets.

There are usually four tongues, two on each side. This set-up allows a player to press against two of the tongues preventing them from contacting the gear, thus producing a softer sound. This is very helpful when dynamics are called for in ratchet parts.

RATCHET PERFORMANCE

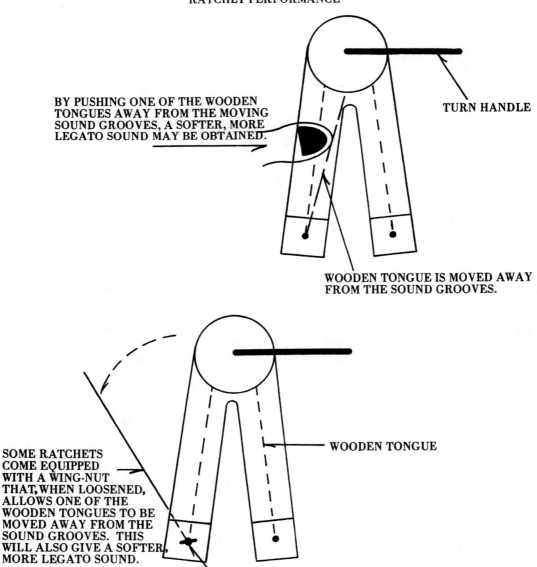

BY PUSHING ONE OF THE WOODEN TONGUES AWAY FROM THE MOVING SOUND GROOVES, A SOFTER, MORE LEGATO SOUND MAY BE OBTAINED.

TURN HANDLE

WOODEN TONGUE IS MOVED AWAY FROM THE SOUND GROOVES.

WOODEN TONGUE

SOME RATCHETS COME EQUIPPED WITH A WING-NUT THAT, WHEN LOOSENED, ALLOWS ONE OF THE WOODEN TONGUES TO BE MOVED AWAY FROM THE SOUND GROOVES. THIS WILL ALSO GIVE A SOFTER, MORE LEGATO SOUND.

WING-NUT

*** HAND CASTANETS ***

The most common type of castanets used in orchestral percussion are the hand castanets. A constant problem with this instrument is the cord connecting the castanets to the handle. If this cord is too loose, the castanets will take too long to make contact, creating unclear rhythms and making fast passages inarticu-late and difficult to play. If the cord is too tight, the castanets will not be able to strike each other to make the proper sound.

Elastic shoestring is the best material to use in tying the castanets together. They can be pulled tightly and tied without losing tension.

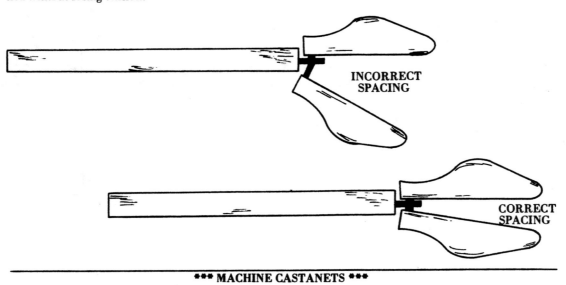

INCORRECT
SPACING

CORRECT
SPACING

*** MACHINE CASTANETS ***

For soft execution of rhythmical passages or parts requiring greater control, use machine castanets. Below is a diagram for constructing a handmade castanet machine.

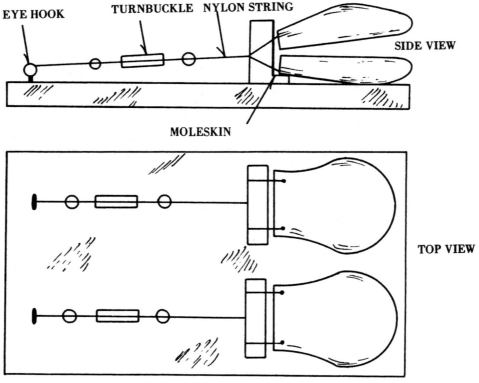

EYE HOOK   TURNBUCKLE NYLON STRING

SIDE VIEW

MOLESKIN

TOP VIEW

66

*** KEYBOARD PERCUSSION INSTRUMENTS ***

The family of keyboard percussion instruments includes: orchestra bells, xylophone, vibraphone, marimba and chimes. Since they all have unique problems, each will be dealt with separately in terms of maintenance and repair.

*** MARIMBA AND XYLOPHONE ***

The marimba and xylophone, having wooden bars and a similar frame, are cared for in the same manner.

*** THE PROPER MALLETS ***

Improper mallets cause much of the damage to wooden bars. The marimba bars, constructed from soft rosewood, cannot stand the punishment of hard rubber or plastic mallets. Yarn-wound, cord-wound or medium and soft rubber mallets are fine.

Since the bars of the xylophone are thicker and the sound must be brighter, a harder mallet is needed. With older rosewood bars, a hard plastic mallet works best. However, since the wood on the newer instruments is considerably softer, a plastic mallet will tend to dent the bar. Therefore, a hard rubber mallet is needed to obtain a bright sound. DO NOT USE A MALLET THAT IS HARDER THAN THE PLAYING SURFACE. Save the hard plastic and rubber mallets for performances. Practicing with a softer mallet increases the life span of the instrument, not to mention the performer's ears!

The xylophone is often over-played dynamically. The timbre of the xylophone will cut through the orchestra without having to be played very hard. Over-playing will not only cause damage to the bars, but it also increases the chances of inaccurate playing.

*** REPAIRING A CRACKED BAR ***

A wooden bar will crack for three reasons:

  1.   Incorrect mallets.
  2.   Excessive use over a long period of time.
  3.   Accidents.

If a surface crack results:

  1.   Sand it smooth so splinters do not develop.
  2.   Apply a small layer of super-glue across the crack.
  3.   This will seal the crack and provide a hard surface to play on.

If the crack appears to be through the bar:

  1.   Continue to split the bar into two pieces without losing any wood.
  2.   Connect the two halves with super-glue.
  3.   Retune as necessary. All tuning should be done by a professional familiar with mallet percussion acoustics.

A few more tips on caring for wooden bar instruments:

  1.   Rosewood will tend to dry out after a period of time. To prevent this from happening, periodically wipe the bars down with a rubbing or penetrating oil. Remove all surface oil after application to prevent it from getting on the mallets.
  2.   Do not store the marimba or xylophone in direct sunlight. This will cause it to go out of tune.
  3.   Protect the instrument by covering it when not in use.

*** RESONATORS ***

Most rattles will develop in the resonators. First check the area where they are riveted together. If the rivet is loose, remove the resonator from the frame and tap lightly on the rivet to wedge it back in place.

Another remedy is to take a piece of moleskin and place it over the rivet. Usually this will hold the rivet against the tube and prevent it from rattling. This same procedure works for preventing rattles caused by the plugs at the bottom of the resonator tubes.

Resonators tend to collect dust, dirt and objects. Periodically, turn them upside down to remove objects. Insert a vacuum hose and thoroughly clean each tube.

RESONATOR TUBE

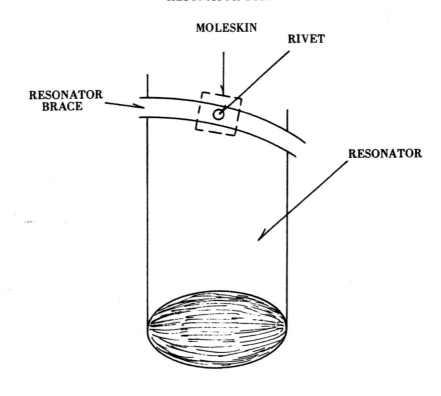

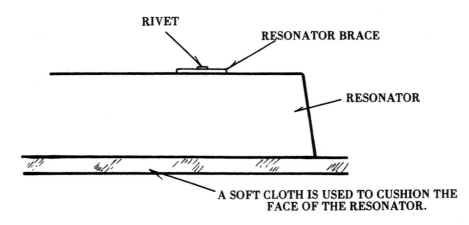

A SOFT CLOTH IS USED TO CUSHION THE
FACE OF THE RESONATOR.

WITH THE RESONATOR LYING FLAT, A SOFT RUBBER-HEADED HAMMER MAY BE USED TO TAP THE RATTLING RIVET, AND RE-SECURE IT TO THE RESONATOR BRACE.

*** THE SUSPENSION CORD ***

The cord and spring suspending each bar needs to be in good repair. The cord should be a mixture of cotton and nylon. Straight cotton cord tends to stretch and does not provide good support for the bars. Clothesline or parachute line cord work well and can be bought at a hardware store.

The springs at the end of the cord should be tight enough to keep the tension necessary for supporting the bars. When restringing the instrument, leave six to eight inches of excess cord which will allow some leverage if it needs to be tightened at a later date.

The suspension posts also need to be checked to be sure they are not touching the bar. An occasional bent post can result from constantly moving the instrument.   As a result, the bar will not vibrate properly and some tone will be lost. To correct this, take a long-nose plier and firmly but slowly bend the post away from the bar.

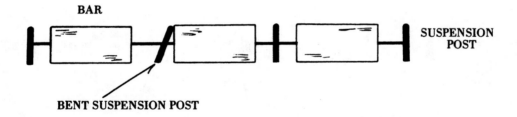

BAR

SUSPENSION
POST

BENT SUSPENSION POST

*** ORCHESTRA BELLS ***

Orchestra bell bars are constructed from steel or brushed aluminum, and unlike wooden bars, are fairly tolerant of damage and weather conditions. The most common problem with this instrument is the buzzing that occurs when the bars are in contact with the frame. The bar can touch the frame in two places: 1.) on the felt where it rests and 2.) the nail or screw attaching each bar.

To increase the resonance of the bars, criss-cross a thin durable cord of gut or monofilament line around the posts so they lie on top of the felt. The bars will then rest on the cord and not on the felt, causing an increase in the sustaining power of the bar.

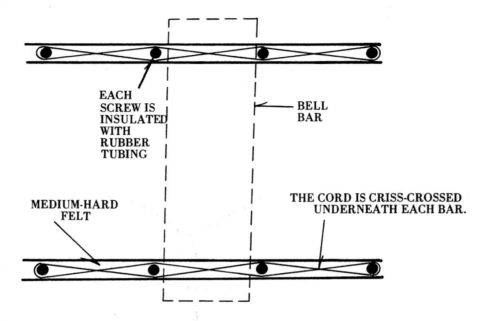

EACH SCREW IS INSULATED WITH RUBBER TUBING

BELL BAR

MEDIUM-HARD FELT

THE CORD IS CRISS-CROSSED UNDERNEATH EACH BAR.

To avoid buzzing, insulate each post with rubber tubing. Windshield washer hose works very well.

For even greater control, replace each post with a similar size screw. This screw should also be insulated. Use of a screw allows for tension adjustment which controls the resonance of each bar.

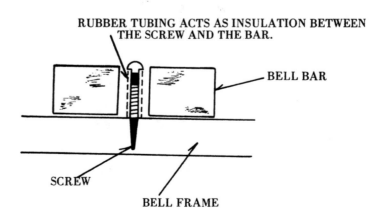

RUBBER TUBING ACTS AS INSULATION BETWEEN THE SCREW AND THE BAR.

BELL BAR

SCREW

BELL FRAME

*** CARE OF BELL BARS ***

Surface rust will appear on the bars if the chrome plating has deteriorated or flaked off. Rub the bar lightly with paste wax to remove most of the surface rust. If they are more severely rusted, a rubbing compound will be necessary. Lightly rub a spot of oil into the bar to inhibit future rusting.

Check the bars for intonation at this point as they may need retuning.

*** BELL STAND ***

Orchestra bells are a heavy instrument and require a solid stand to support them. If an adjustable metal stand is used, secure a hose clamp on the shaft of the stand to prevent slipping.

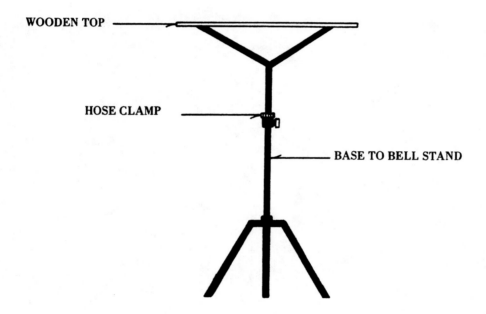

WOODEN TOP

HOSE CLAMP

BASE TO BELL STAND

The following suggestions are recommended for proper maintenance of the vibraphone:

1. Keep the bars clean with a moist chamois cloth.
2. Periodically, oil the motor and the revolving shaft in the resonators to insure a smooth, quiet operation.
3. The electrical cord should be checked for fraying or loose wires.
4. To correct a squeaky pedal, apply powdered graphite to the problem areas. USE SPARINGLY!
5. Occasionally, the damper bar will not stop all the sound when applied. A flat spot can develop on the felt, preventing it from properly dampening the bar. To correct, take a curved carpet needle and lightly pull up on the top layer of felt. This will increase the height of the felt, and allow it to reach the bar.
6. A spare pulley belt is good to have in your stick bag. If the belt becomes worn or breaks, it can easily be repaired. Take the two ends of the belt and cut them at angles to each other. Then, using super-glue, cement the two sections together.

REPAIRING A VIBRAPHONE BELT

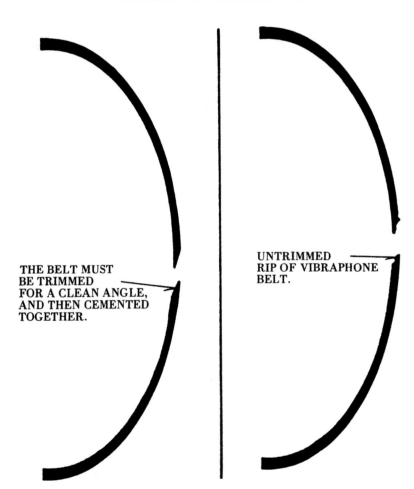

THE BELT MUST BE TRIMMED FOR A CLEAN ANGLE, AND THEN CEMENTED TOGETHER.

UNTRIMMED RIP OF VIBRAPHONE BELT.

7. Place the pedal of the vibraphone (chimes also) in the upright position when transporting. The pedal is subject to damage in the lowered position and can be bent out of shape.
8. Check the suspension cord regularly. Since the bars are made of metal, the edges do tend to cut into the cord more easily than a wooden bar.
9. For those players who find the normal height of the keyboard percussion instruments uncomfortable, raise the instrument to a more desirable height by inserting a 2" by 4" block of wood under each caster.

A 2" BY 4" BLOCK UNDER EACH CASTER WILL RAISE THE INSTRUMENT TO A COMFORTABLE PLAYING HEIGHT.
A RAISED RIDGE AROUND THE EDGE OF THE BLOCK WILL KEEP THE CASTER FROM MOVING OFF OF THE BLOCK.

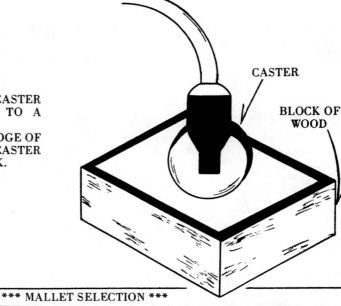

CASTER

BLOCK OF WOOD

*** MALLET SELECTION ***

TYPE OF MALLET	BELLS	VIBES	XYLO.	MARIMBA	CHIMES
YARN WOUND		●		●	
CORD WOUND		●	●	●	
SOFT RUBBER		●		●	
HARD RUBBER	●		●		
PLASTIC	●		●		●
BRASS	●				
ROSEWOOD			●	●	
RAWHIDE					●

Listed above are the most common types of mallets used on the keyboard percussion instruments. Always use the proper mallet on the proper instrument to avoid damage to the bars.

*** SPECIAL STICKS AND MALLETS ***

Sticks and mallets are the tools of the percussionist's trade. Performers choose mallets very carefully because they become a very personal part of their equipment.

Equally important is the case or bag used to transport and store these mallets. There are a number of stick bags and attache cases commercially available. The case is also important for protecting the mallets from dirt and moisture.

The following section lists a number of specialized mallets all serious percussionists should consider including as part of their equipment.

*** GONG OR TAM TAM BEATER ***

The secret of an effective gong beater is one that provides ample weight (or mass) to quickly set the large tam tam in motion.

The following instructions will help in constructing a basic gong beater:

1. Obtain a heavy wooden handle with a diameter of approximately 1 1/2 inches.
2. Two rubber hockey pucks, cemented together, form a good base for the head.
3. Drill the proper size hole in the hockey pucks to accommodate the handle.
4. Wrap a piece of felt or moleskin around the outer section of the pucks.
5. Yarn or cord can now be wrapped around the felt to a desired thickness.

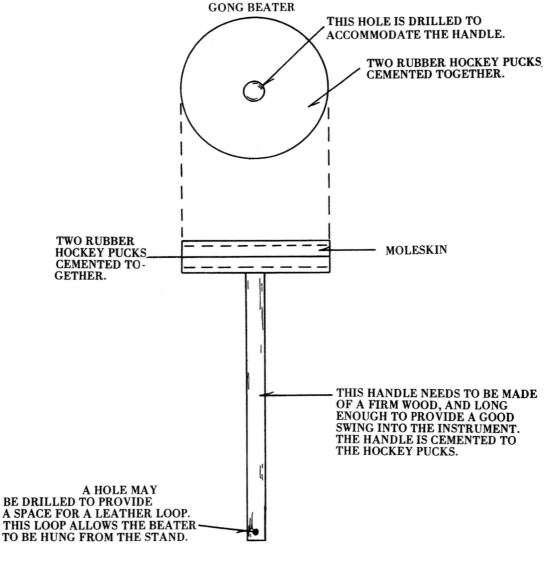

GONG BEATER

THIS HOLE IS DRILLED TO ACCOMMODATE THE HANDLE.

TWO RUBBER HOCKEY PUCKS, CEMENTED TOGETHER.

TWO RUBBER HOCKEY PUCKS CEMENTED TO-GETHER.

MOLESKIN

THIS HANDLE NEEDS TO BE MADE OF A FIRM WOOD, AND LONG ENOUGH TO PROVIDE A GOOD SWING INTO THE INSTRUMENT. THE HANDLE IS CEMENTED TO THE HOCKEY PUCKS.

A HOLE MAY BE DRILLED TO PROVIDE A SPACE FOR A LEATHER LOOP. THIS LOOP ALLOWS THE BEATER TO BE HUNG FROM THE STAND.

*** RUTE ***

Rute is a German word for a switch, or a bunch of twigs tied together. Mahler uses this quite often in his Symphonic works. The rute is used in place of a bass drum beater and can be played on the bass drum head or shell.

Simply cut a bunch of twigs, two to three-feet long, and bind them together at one end to make a handle. Tie the ends together with plastic electrician's tape.

The ideal time to obtain the twigs is during the pruning season (winter months). Fruit trees provide a good supply. Brushes are now available made with a long, heavy plastic fan. These can also be used for a rute. The sound may not be as heavy as a bunch of twigs, but is more durable and easier to store.

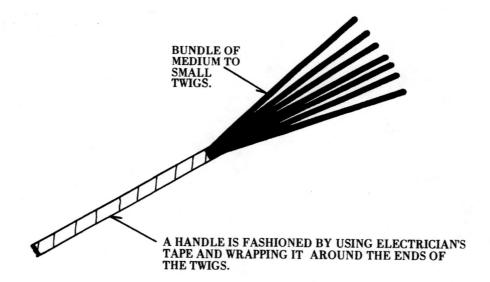

BUNDLE OF
MEDIUM TO
SMALL
TWIGS.

A HANDLE IS FASHIONED BY USING ELECTRICIAN'S
TAPE AND WRAPPING IT AROUND THE ENDS OF
THE TWIGS.

*** DOUBLE HEADED STICKS ***

1. Begin with a standard pair of orchestral snare drum sticks.
2. With masking tape, wrap the butt end of the sticks several times until a large head is built up.
3. Apply a layer of moleskin around the masking tape.

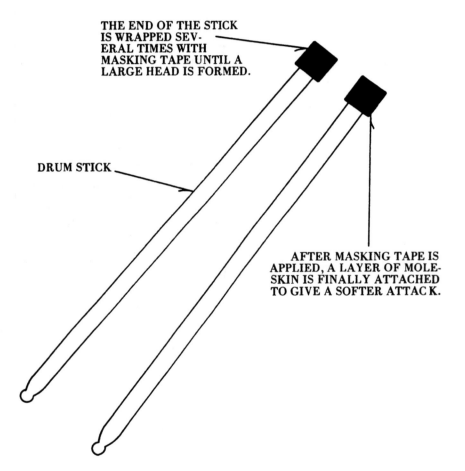

THE END OF THE STICK IS WRAPPED SEVERAL TIMES WITH MASKING TAPE UNTIL A LARGE HEAD IS FORMED.

DRUM STICK

AFTER MASKING TAPE IS APPLIED, A LAYER OF MOLESKIN IS FINALLY ATTACHED TO GIVE A SOFTER ATTACK.

*** NON—RETRACTABLE BRUSHES ***

1. Purchase a non-retractable pair of brushes with a wooden handle.
2. Attach a metal ring to the base of the dowel. The ring can be any small-diametered metal that is easily bent into a circular shape. This is very handy when using brushes as a double-headed beater on snare drum, triangle or cymbals.
3. For a more controlled sound, attach a small piece of tape to the base of the brush narrowing the overall spread.

BRUSH WITH ATTACHED METAL RING

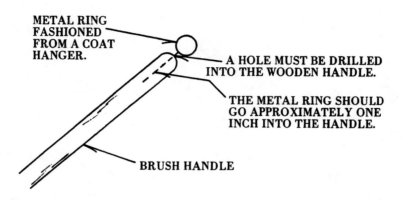

METAL RING FASHIONED FROM A COAT HANGER.

A HOLE MUST BE DRILLED INTO THE WOODEN HANDLE.

THE METAL RING SHOULD GO APPROXIMATELY ONE INCH INTO THE HANDLE.

BRUSH HANDLE

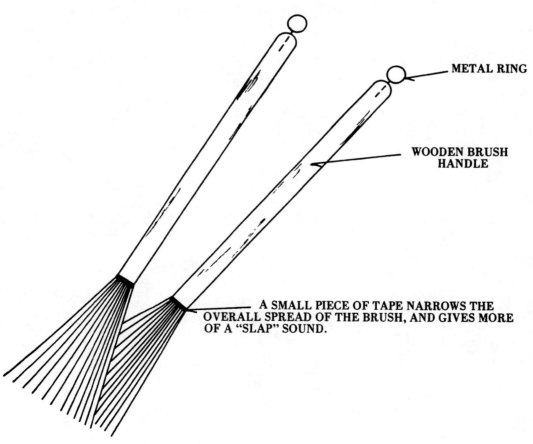

METAL RING

WOODEN BRUSH HANDLE

A SMALL PIECE OF TAPE NARROWS THE OVERALL SPREAD OF THE BRUSH, AND GIVES MORE OF A "SLAP" SOUND.

*** MARIMBA MALLET VARIATIONS ***

Cover the head of the mallet with a piece of plastic wrap. Secure at the base with electrical tape. A "slap" effect can be heard by using this technique.

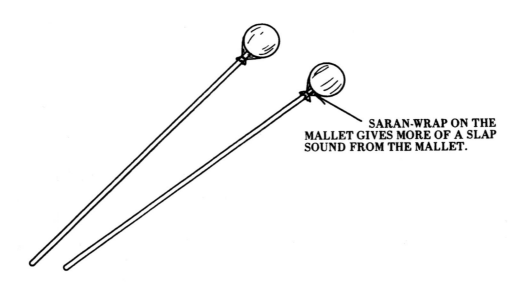

SARAN-WRAP ON THE MALLET GIVES MORE OF A SLAP SOUND FROM THE MALLET.

Wrapping a piece of moleskin on a rubber-headed mallet will give it more of a legato sound.

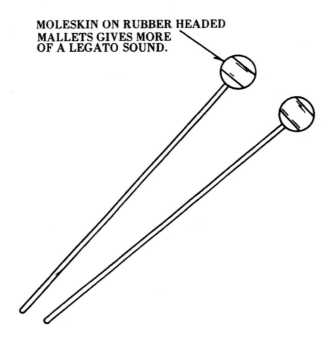

MOLESKIN ON RUBBER HEADED MALLETS GIVES MORE OF A LEGATO SOUND.

*** MALLET RACK ***

Below is a simple diagram for an on-stage mallet rack.

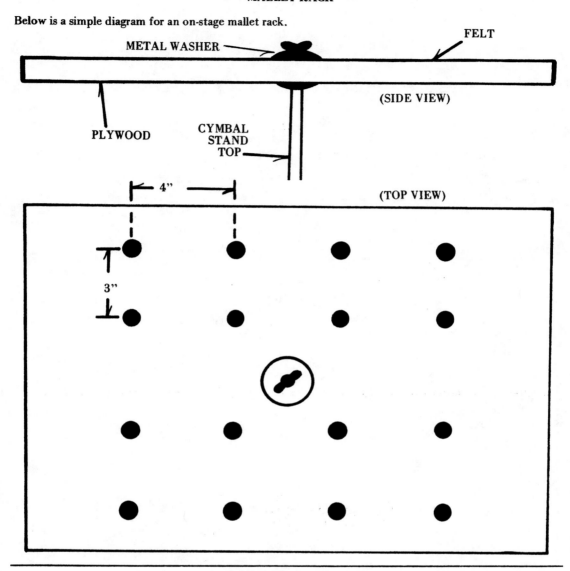

*** SURVIVAL REPAIR KIT ***

The following items are suggested for your Survival Repair Kit. A small tackle box will hold all of this equipment. Most emergencies can be met on the job with the materials listed below:

DRUM KEY	THUMB TACKS	SUPER GLUE
TIMPANI KEY	SPARE VIBRAPHONE BELT	WING–NUTS
SCREWDRIVER (standard & Phillips)	DUCT TAPE	RUBBER SLEEVES
KNIFE (X-acto)	MASKING TAPE/TEFLON TAPE	RUBBER TUBING
NEEDLES (curved & straight)	PENCILS & MARKING PENS	FELTS (washers)
NEEDLE–NOSE PLIERS	SCISSORS	SHEET FELT
DRAWING COMPASS	MOLESKIN	VASOLINE
RULER (tape measure)	MATCHES	PARAFFIN WAX
C–CLAMPS	GUT (various weights)	SAND PAPER
STRING	UN–WAXED DENTAL FLOSS	WASHERS (metal)
POWDERED GRAPHITE	RUBBER CEMENT	WOOD GLUE
3–IN–ONE OIL	RUBBER BANDS	

*** SOUND PROJECTION FOR MARCHING DRUMS ***

*** SNARE AND TENOR DRUMS ***

MARCHING SNARE DRUM SOUND PROJECTION

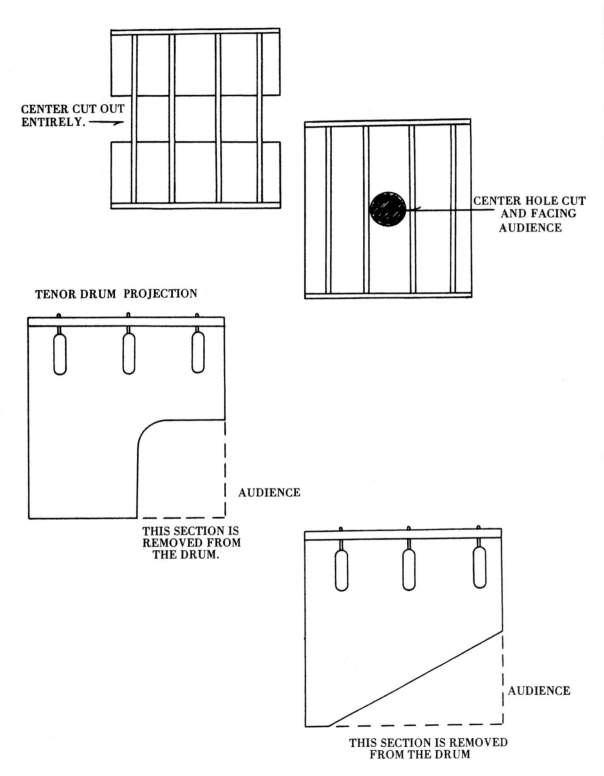

CENTER CUT OUT ENTIRELY. →

CENTER HOLE CUT AND FACING AUDIENCE

TENOR DRUM PROJECTION

AUDIENCE

THIS SECTION IS REMOVED FROM THE DRUM.

AUDIENCE

THIS SECTION IS REMOVED FROM THE DRUM

*** SOUND PROJECTORS ***

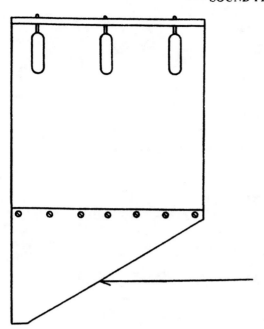
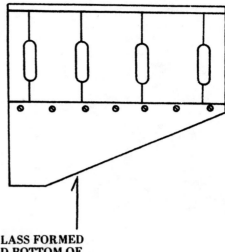

PLEXIGLASS FORMED
AROUND BOTTOM OF
SHELL AND BOLTED
TO DRUM.

*** MULTIDRUM SET—UPS (MARCHING) ***

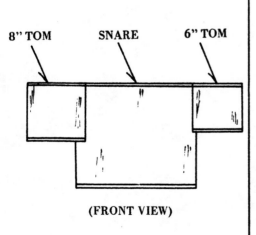

8" TOM   SNARE   6" TOM

(FRONT VIEW)

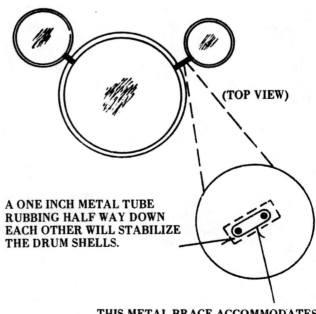

(TOP VIEW)

A ONE INCH METAL TUBE
RUBBING HALF WAY DOWN
EACH OTHER WILL STABILIZE
THE DRUM SHELLS.

THIS METAL BRACE ACCOMMODATES
THE TOP LUGS FROM EACH DRUM
AND STABILIZES THE DRUMS FROM
THE TOP.

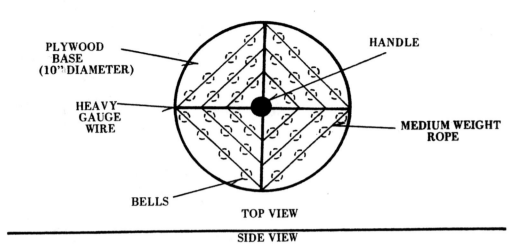

PLYWOOD BASE (10" DIAMETER)

HANDLE

HEAVY GAUGE WIRE

MEDIUM WEIGHT ROPE

BELLS

TOP VIEW

SIDE VIEW

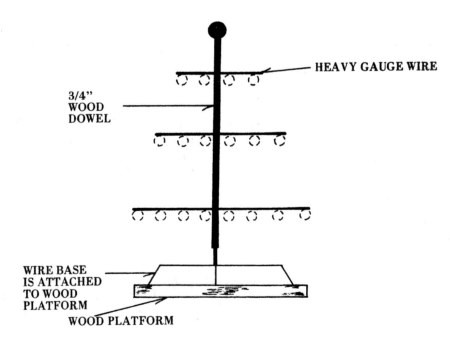

HEAVY GAUGE WIRE

3/4" WOOD DOWEL

WIRE BASE IS ATTACHED TO WOOD PLATFORM

WOOD PLATFORM

BY GRASPING THE CENTER HANDLE AND GENTLY MOVING IT FROM SIDE TO SIDE, A LIGHT, FLOWING BELL SOUND CAN BE ATTAINED.

*** BELL/BUZZER EFFECT BOX ***

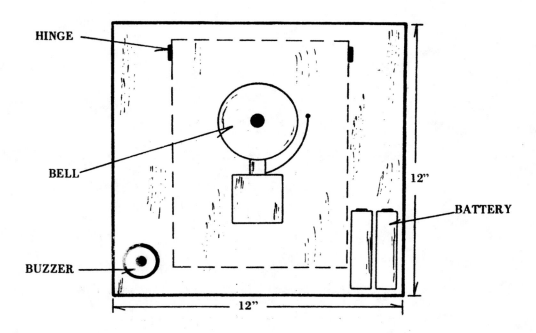

HINGE

BELL

BUZZER

BATTERY

12"

12"

WITH THE BUZZER PRESSED, GRADUALLY OPEN THE BOX LID, THUS INCREASING THE VOLUME OF SOUND. AS THE LID IS PUT BACK DOWN, THE VOLUME WILL DECREASE.

TOP VIEW

SIDE VIEW

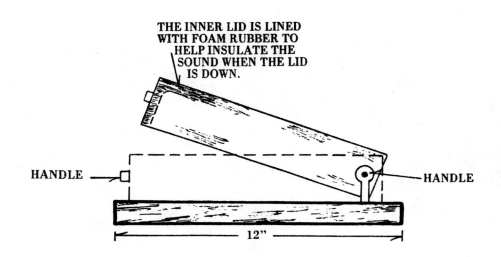

THE INNER LID IS LINED WITH FOAM RUBBER TO HELP INSULATE THE SOUND WHEN THE LID IS DOWN.

HANDLE

HANDLE

12"

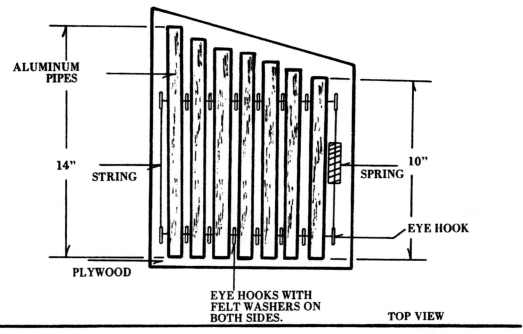

ALUMINUM
PIPES

14"

STRING

PLYWOOD

EYE HOOKS WITH
FELT WASHERS ON
BOTH SIDES.

SPRING

10"

EYE HOOK

TOP VIEW

SIDE VIEW

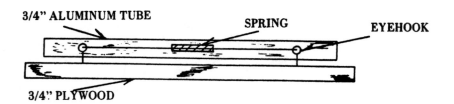

3/4" ALUMINUM TUBE

SPRING

EYEHOOK

3/4" PLYWOOD

THE SEVEN TONE PIPE RACK IS A SPECIALTY INSTRUMENT CALLED FOR BY LOU HARRISON FOR PERFORMANCE OF HIS " FUGUE FOR PERCUSSION". TUBING CUT AT VARIOUS LENGTHS AND PLAYED WITH A RUBBER MALLET WORKS WELL FOR THIS.

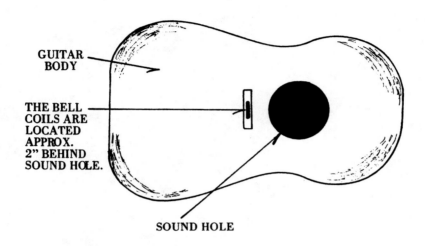

GUITAR
BODY

THE BELL
COILS ARE
LOCATED
APPROX.
2" BEHIND
SOUND HOLE.

SOUND HOLE

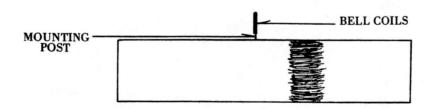

BELL COILS

MOUNTING
POST

ALSO CALLED FOR IN HARRISON'S " FUGUE" ARE BELL COILS. THE GUITAR BODY
ACTS AS THE RESONATING CHAMBER WHEN THE COILS ARE STRUCK. THE COILS
ARE AVAILABLE FROM CLOCK STORES, AND ARE USED IN LARGE GRANDFATHER
CLOCKS. THEY SHOULD BE PLAYED WITH MEDIUM-HARD MALLETS.

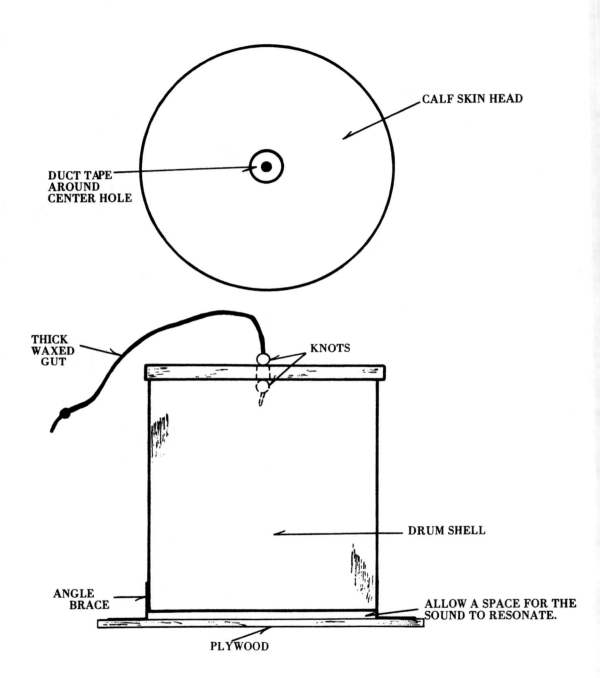

CALF SKIN HEAD

DUCT TAPE
AROUND
CENTER HOLE

THICK
WAXED
GUT

KNOTS

DRUM SHELL

ANGLE
BRACE

ALLOW A SPACE FOR THE
SOUND TO RESONATE.

PLYWOOD

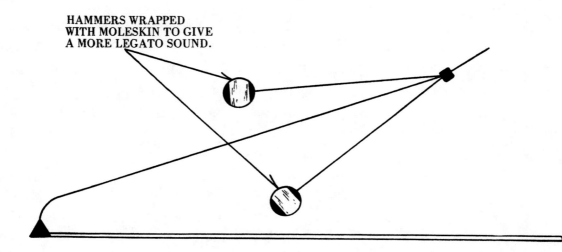

HAMMERS WRAPPED
WITH MOLESKIN TO GIVE
A MORE LEGATO SOUND.

*** DAMPER BAR FOR MARK TREE ***

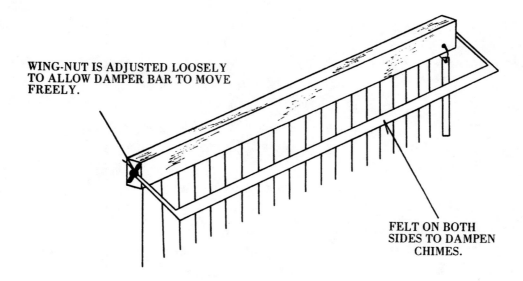

WING-NUT IS ADJUSTED LOOSELY
TO ALLOW DAMPER BAR TO MOVE
FREELY.

FELT ON BOTH
SIDES TO DAMPEN
CHIMES.

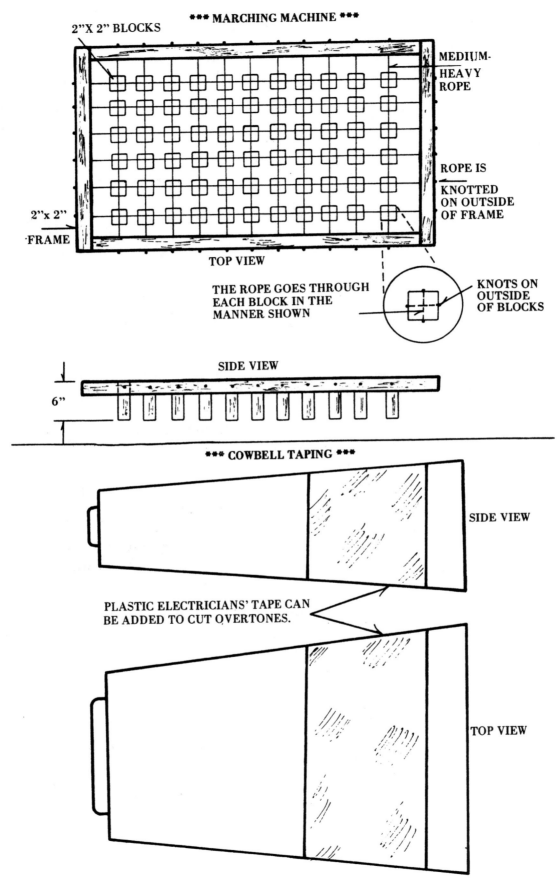

*** MARCHING MACHINE ***

2"X 2" BLOCKS

MEDIUM-
HEAVY
ROPE

ROPE IS
KNOTTED
ON OUTSIDE
OF FRAME

2"x 2"
FRAME

TOP VIEW

THE ROPE GOES THROUGH
EACH BLOCK IN THE
MANNER SHOWN

KNOTS ON
OUTSIDE
OF BLOCKS

SIDE VIEW

6"

*** COWBELL TAPING ***

SIDE VIEW

PLASTIC ELECTRICIANS' TAPE CAN
BE ADDED TO CUT OVERTONES.

TOP VIEW

INSIDE OF THE RESONATING CHAMBER SHOULD BE COATED
WITH VARNISH TO HELP THE SOUND RESONATE.

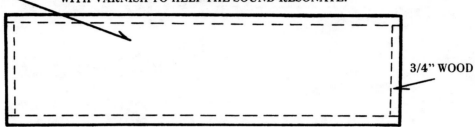

3/4" WOOD

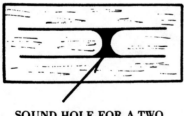

SOUND HOLE FOR A TWO
TONE SOUND BOARD.

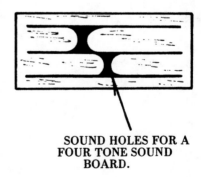

SOUND HOLES FOR A
FOUR TONE SOUND
BOARD.

*** SLAPSTICK ***

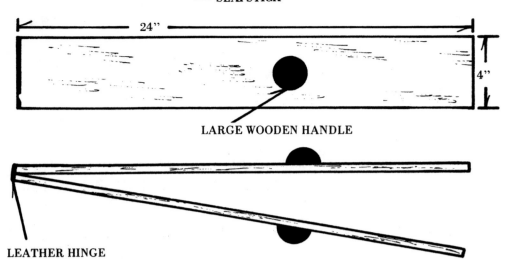

LARGE WOODEN HANDLE

LEATHER HINGE

THE SLAPSTICK WORKS BEST WHEN THE HANDLES ARE LOCATED SLIGHTLY OFF-CENTER, AND CLOSER TO THE OPEN END. THIS ALLOWS FOR MORE POWERFUL PLAYING. ALSO, A THIN COAT OF PAINT, APPLIED TO THE INSIDE OF EACH PADDLE, WILL GIVE A MORE STACCATO SOUND.

*** MALLET AND ACCESSORY RACK ***

MALLET INSTRUMENT

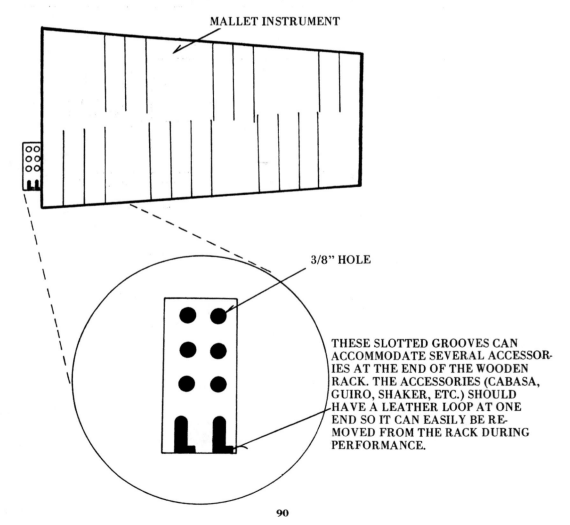

3/8" HOLE

THESE SLOTTED GROOVES CAN ACCOMMODATE SEVERAL ACCESSOR-IES AT THE END OF THE WOODEN RACK. THE ACCESSORIES (CABASA, GUIRO, SHAKER, ETC.) SHOULD HAVE A LEATHER LOOP AT ONE END SO IT CAN EASILY BE RE-MOVED FROM THE RACK DURING PERFORMANCE.

*** MULTIPLE COWBELL HOLDER ***

FELT   1/4" HOLE TO ACCOMMODATE U—CLAMP

COWBELL

METAL PLATE

PLYWOOD

3/8"
ROD

SIDE VIEW

*** SINGLE WOODBLOCK HOLDER ***

WOODBLOCK

MEDIUM
HEAVY WIRE

EYEHOOK

MOLESKIN

PLYWOOD BASE

WING NUT

3/8" HEX NUT

3/8" ROD

SIDE VIEW

*** DOUBLE WOODBLOCK HOLDER ***

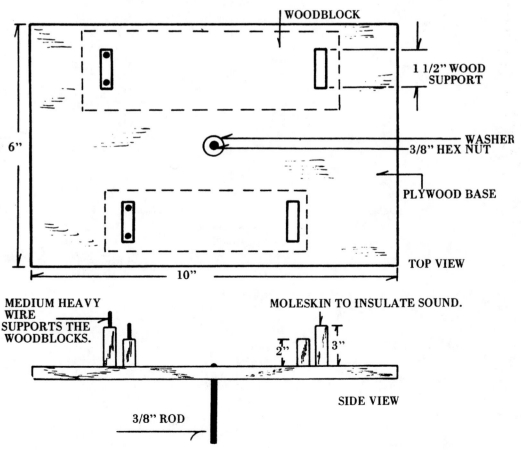

WOODBLOCK

1 1/2" WOOD
SUPPORT

6"

WASHER
3/8" HEX NUT

PLYWOOD BASE

TOP VIEW

10"

MEDIUM HEAVY
WIRE
SUPPORTS THE
WOODBLOCKS.

MOLESKIN TO INSULATE SOUND.

2"   3"

SIDE VIEW

3/8" ROD

91

*** CHIME RACK ***

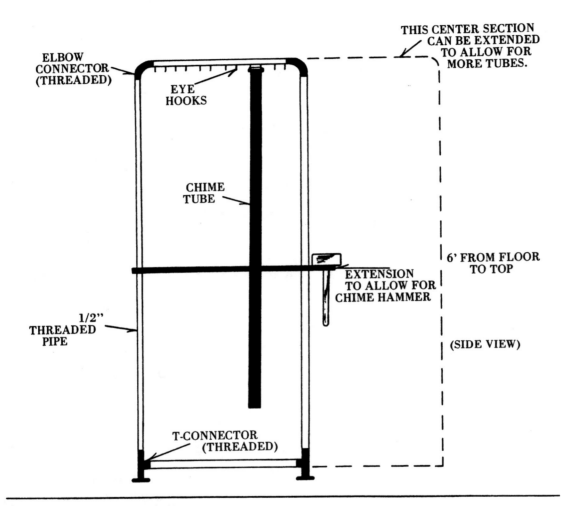

ELBOW
CONNECTOR
(THREADED)

EYE
HOOKS

THIS CENTER SECTION
CAN BE EXTENDED
TO ALLOW FOR
MORE TUBES.

CHIME
TUBE

EXTENSION
TO ALLOW FOR
CHIME HAMMER

6' FROM FLOOR
TO TOP

1/2"
THREADED
PIPE

(SIDE VIEW)

T-CONNECTOR
(THREADED)

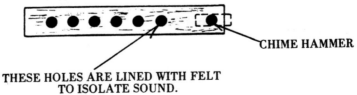

CHIME HAMMER

THESE HOLES ARE LINED WITH FELT
TO ISOLATE SOUND.

(TOP VIEW)

*** HORIZONTAL SLEIGH BELL RACK ***

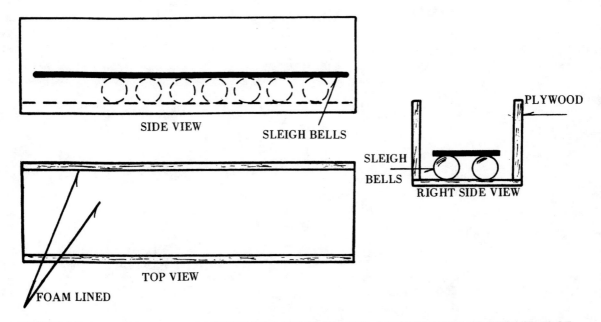

SIDE VIEW

SLEIGH BELLS

PLYWOOD

SLEIGH
BELLS

RIGHT SIDE VIEW

TOP VIEW

FOAM LINED

SLEIGH BELLS ARE A PROBLEM WHEN NOT BEING PLAYED AS THEY TEND TO CREATE ALOT OF EXTRA SOUND FROM RATTLING. WITH THE SLEIGH BELLS IN THE HORIZONTAL AND/OR VERTICAL SLEIGH BELL RACK, THIS UNWANTED SOUND WILL BE KEPT TO A MINIMUM.

*** VERTICAL SLEIGH BELL RACK ***

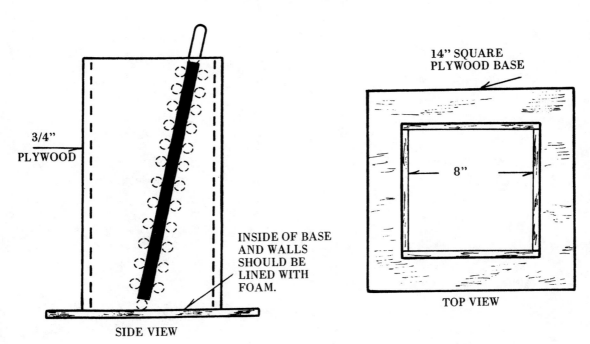

3/4"
PLYWOOD

14" SQUARE
PLYWOOD BASE

8"

INSIDE OF BASE
AND WALLS
SHOULD BE
LINED WITH
FOAM.

SIDE VIEW

TOP VIEW

*** A DEVICE FOR RE-FLUFFING TIMPANI FELT ***

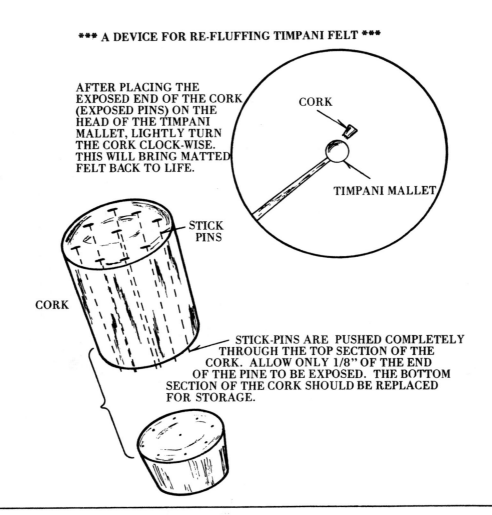

AFTER PLACING THE EXPOSED END OF THE CORK (EXPOSED PINS) ON THE HEAD OF THE TIMPANI MALLET, LIGHTLY TURN THE CORK CLOCK-WISE. THIS WILL BRING MATTED FELT BACK TO LIFE.

CORK

TIMPANI MALLET

STICK PINS

CORK

STICK-PINS ARE PUSHED COMPLETELY THROUGH THE TOP SECTION OF THE CORK. ALLOW ONLY 1/8" OF THE END OF THE PINE TO BE EXPOSED. THE BOTTOM SECTION OF THE CORK SHOULD BE REPLACED FOR STORAGE.

*** CHAIN-DRUM TUNING GAUGE ***

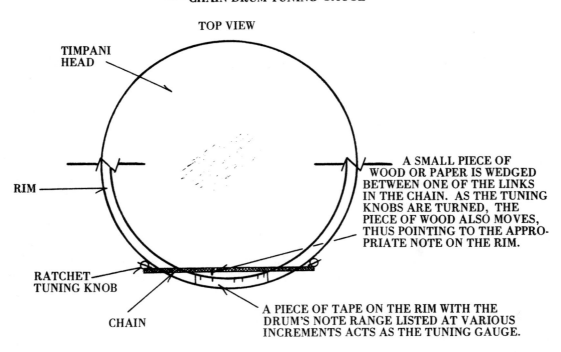

TOP VIEW

TIMPANI HEAD

RIM

A SMALL PIECE OF WOOD OR PAPER IS WEDGED BETWEEN ONE OF THE LINKS IN THE CHAIN. AS THE TUNING KNOBS ARE TURNED, THE PIECE OF WOOD ALSO MOVES, THUS POINTING TO THE APPROPRIATE NOTE ON THE RIM.

RATCHET TUNING KNOB

CHAIN

A PIECE OF TAPE ON THE RIM WITH THE DRUM'S NOTE RANGE LISTED AT VARIOUS INCREMENTS ACTS AS THE TUNING GAUGE.

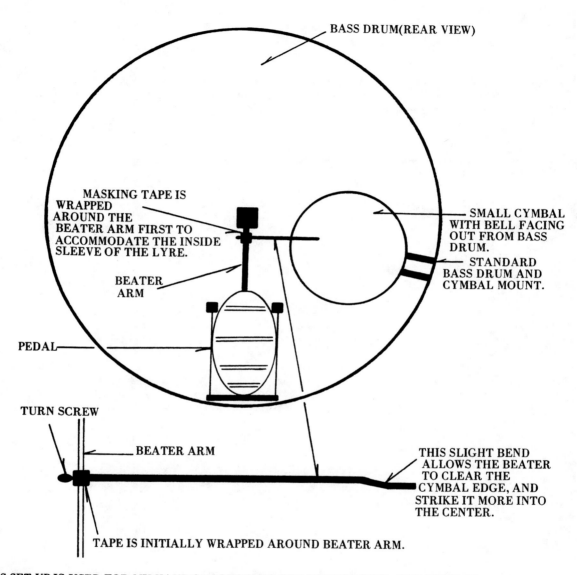

BASS DRUM(REAR VIEW)

MASKING TAPE IS WRAPPED AROUND THE BEATER ARM FIRST TO ACCOMMODATE THE INSIDE SLEEVE OF THE LYRE.

BEATER ARM

SMALL CYMBAL WITH BELL FACING OUT FROM BASS DRUM.

STANDARD BASS DRUM AND CYMBAL MOUNT.

PEDAL

TURN SCREW

BEATER ARM

THIS SLIGHT BEND ALLOWS THE BEATER TO CLEAR THE CYMBAL EDGE, AND STRIKE IT MORE INTO THE CENTER.

TAPE IS INITIALLY WRAPPED AROUND BEATER ARM.

THIS SET-UP IS USED FOR MILHAUD'S "CONCERTO FOR PERCUSSION". THE PIECE OF METAL ATTACHED TO THE BEATER ARM IS A MARCHING LYRE FOR A TROMBONE. THE LYRE GIVES THE CORRECT LENGTH, ALONG WITH A TURN SCREW, WHICH ENABLES THE PERFORMER TO MOVE THE LYRE AWAY FROM THE CYMBAL. THIS IS NECESSARY FOR THE FINAL MOVEMENT OF THE CONCERTO.

THE ALLEN WRENCH MAY HAVE THE ANGLE SAWED OFF TO ACCOMMODATE THE INSERTION OF THE SPUR FROM THE OUTSIDE OF THE BASS DRUM. IF THIS ANGLE IS LEFT ON, THE SPUR MAY BE INSERTED FROM THE INSIDE.

THE END OF THE SPUR SHOULD BE GROUND TO A POINT.

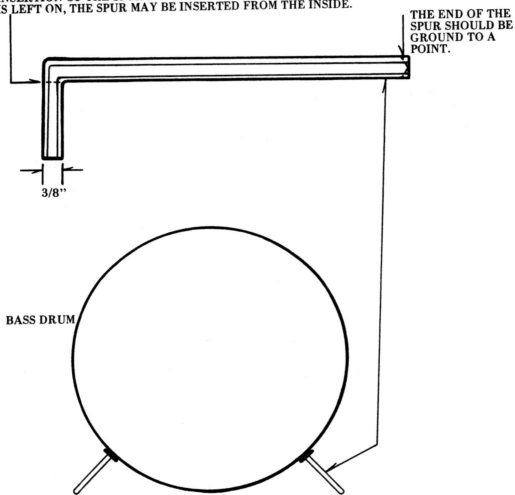

3/8"

BASS DRUM

SEVERAL DRUM COMPANIES HAVE BASS DRUM SPURS THAT ARE HEXAGONAL IN SHAPE. EVEN THOUGH THIS PARTICULAR DESIGN IS NO LONGER bEING MANU-FACTURED, MANY OF THESE DRUMS ARE STILL BEING USED THAT REQUIRE THIS TYPE OF SPUR. A 3/8" ALLEN WRENCH WORKS WELL FOR A SUBSTITUTE IF THIS SPUR SHOULD NEED TO BE REPLACED.

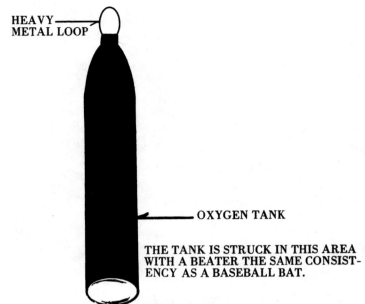

HEAVY
METAL LOOP

OXYGEN TANK

THE TANK IS STRUCK IN THIS AREA
WITH A BEATER THE SAME CONSIST-
ENCY AS A BASEBALL BAT.

THESE OXYGEN BELLS ARE USED IN MANY CONTEMPORARY SETTINGS WHERE LARGE
CHURCH BELL EFFECTS ARE DESIRED. (MANY LOU HARRISON WORKS AND H. OWEN
REED'S "LA FIESTA MEXICANA").

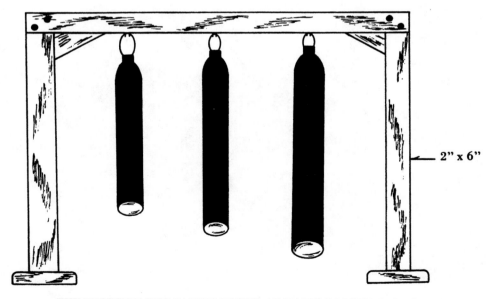

2" x 6"

THE EMPTY TANKS CAN BE SAWED AT VARIOUS LENGTHS TO
SIMULATE DIFFERENT TONES.

*** TRIANGLE TREE ***

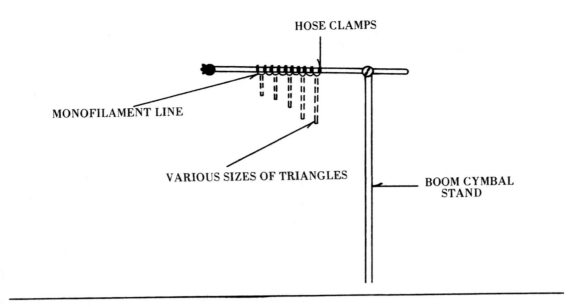

HOSE CLAMPS

MONOFILAMENT LINE

VARIOUS SIZES OF TRIANGLES

BOOM CYMBAL
STAND

*** MULTIPLE TRIANGLE RACK ***

HOLES ARE DRILLED COMPLETELY THROUGH THE STEEL
ROD TO ACCOMMODATE THE MONOFILAMENT LINE.

14"

(TOP VIEW)

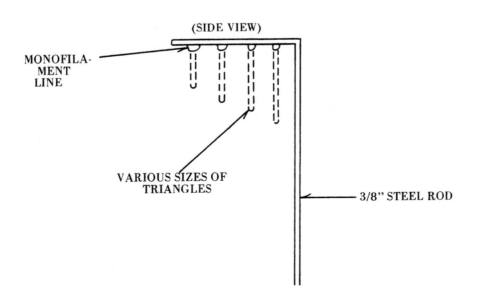

(SIDE VIEW)

MONOFILA-
MENT
LINE

VARIOUS SIZES OF
TRIANGLES

3/8" STEEL ROD

*** USING STICKS ON THE TAMBOURINE ***

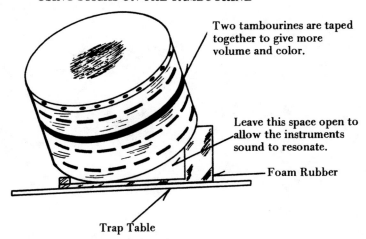

Two tambourines are taped together to give more volume and color.

Leave this space open to allow the instruments sound to resonate.

Foam Rubber

Trap Table

This idea is useful for pieces such as "Pines of Rome", where the tambourine player must perform using **snare drum sticks.** For best results, the two tambourines should have different jingles, such as German silver **and hammered bronze.** This will increase the color of the sound. The jingles, however, should not be heavy **as they will not react quickly to the snare drum stick.**

*** SUSPENDING METAL BELL PLATES ***

A wooden dowel, notched at each end, keeps the cord from vibrating against the metal plate.

Clip

Clip

Cord or Gut

wooden dowel

1/8" Hole

FRONT VIEW

SIDE VIEW

A thinner plate usually increases the resonance.

The 1/8" hole is drilled at the nodal point of the plate. (i.e.- the point of least resonance).